Brexit and British Politics

BREXIT
AND
BRITISH
POLITICS

———

Geoffrey Evans
Anand Menon

polity

The right of Geoffrey Evans, Anand Menon to be identified as Authors of this Work has been asserted in accordance with the UK Copyright, Designs and Patents Act 1988.

First published in 2017 by Polity Press

Polity Press
65 Bridge Street
Cambridge CB2 1UR, UK

Polity Press
101 Station Landing
Suite 300
Medford, MA 02155, USA

ISBN-13: 978-1-5095-2385-6
ISBN-13: 978-1-5095-2386-3 (paperback)

A catalogue record for this book is available from the British Library.

Typeset in 11 on 14 pt Sabon by
Servis Filmsetting Ltd, Stockport, Cheshire
Printed and bound in Great Britain by CPI Group (UK) Ltd, Croyden

The publisher has used its best endeavours to ensure that the URLs for external websites referred to in this book are correct and active at the time of going to press. However, the publisher has no responsibility for the websites and can make no guarantee that a site will remain live or that the content is or will remain appropriate.

Every effort has been made to trace all copyright holders, but if any have been inadvertently overlooked the publisher will be pleased to include any necessary credits in any subsequent reprint or edition.

For further information on Polity, visit our website: politybooks.com

Contents

Figures and Table

Acknowledgements

In writing this book, both of us have drawn on help and support from many sources.

Geoff would like to thank the Economic and Social Research Council (ESRC) for funding the EU Referendum waves of the British Election Study (BES), and his colleagues in that study for their insights. Particular thanks to Jon Mellon, Chris Prosser and Noah Carl for their input. A special thanks also to those people in Stoke and North Staffordshire who gave him views on Brexit that were refreshingly different from those that could be found in the Senior Common Room.

Anand would also like to express his gratitude to the ESRC for trusting him with the Directorship of the UK in a Changing Europe initiative, and to Ben Miller, Phoebe Couzens and Navjyot Lehl for effectively running it while he was writing this book. He's had the privilege of working with some of the best scholars in the business, from whom he has learnt a great deal. Special thanks in this regard to Catherine Barnard and Jonathan Portes, both leaders in their respective fields and both valued friends. They will doubtless recognise

Acknowledgements

in the pages that follow many of the things they have taught me. Camilla Macdonald and Jack Glynn provided invaluable research assistance, without which this book would not have appeared before we left the European Union. Finally, Leigh Mueller was a remarkably fast and ridiculously patient copy-editor. At Polity, grateful thanks to Louise Knight, who, from the first coffee in Pret, has proved relentless in both believing in the project and insisting that the manuscript was finished (more or less) on time.

We dedicate the book to our partners, Julia and Nicola, who, after all, have had to tolerate its intrusion in their lives for far too long.

Preface:
That Was a Year, That Was

The lack of referendum was poisoning British politics, and I put that right.

David Cameron, April 2017[1]

At 4.39 a.m. on Friday 24 June 2016, David Dimbleby appeared on our television screens to announce that the people of the UK had voted to leave the European Union. The British people had rejected the advice of their political establishment, of experts both foreign and home-grown. They had confounded academics and commentators alike by rejecting the status quo and voting for change.

The result generated plenty of hyperbolic comment. And hyperbole, was, unusually, not wholly out of place. This was, after all, the first state-wide referendum in which the electorate had rejected the advice of the government. It was described by the BBC's Andrew Marr as the 'biggest democratic rebellion in modern British history'.[2]

Politicians and pundits alike were taken by surprise. Nigel Farage, leader of the United Kingdom

Independence Party (UKIP), had conceded defeat as the polls closed. And one of us was in a BBC radio studio to hear John Redwood effectively do likewise an hour or so later. Andrew Cooper, David Cameron's pollster, had predicted a win for the Remain camp by 10 points on the day of the vote itself. Meanwhile, financial markets had blithely ignored the possibility of Brexit. Between the polls closing and the announcement of the result, the pound fell 10 per cent against the dollar – a slide larger than those that had accompanied both the financial crisis of 2008 and sterling's departure from the European Exchange Rate Mechanism in 1992.

That the referendum was a defining moment in the political history of the country seemed clear enough at the time. On the morning of the result, a harried political editor of one of the quality broadsheets could be heard on College Green, opposite the Palace of Westminster, breathlessly proclaiming that 'the Prime Minister has just resigned, and it's only the third story on our website'.

David Cameron's departure, moreover, was soon followed by a leadership challenge against the Labour leader of the opposition and the resignation of Nigel Farage as leader of UKIP. British politics was changing.

Mr Cameron's successor in 10 Downing Street was quick to emphasize that she saw the Referendum as the beginning, not the end, of that process of change. From her first statement as Prime Minister, Theresa May made it clear that Brexit marked a break in our politics. Standing outside her new front door on 13 July, she declared her intention to make Britain 'a country that works for everyone', driven by the interests of those 'just about managing' rather than those of the 'privileged few'. Launching her Plan for Britain in March 2017, she was more explicit still, remarking that the 'EU referendum result was an instruction to change the way our country works, and the people for whom it works, forever'.

It was in part her desire to bring this about that led to her ill-fated decision to call a snap General Election for 8 June 2017. We all know what happened then. After a disastrous campaign, she squandered an overwhelming lead in the polls and ended up with a minority government in place of the slim majority that had so frustrated her. The outcome illustrated all too clearly that Brexit's political impact was far from over.

Indeed, the potentially profound long-term implications of that Referendum are now clearer – albeit still profoundly indistinct – than they were in its immediate aftermath. There were signs, in that recent election, of a real 'Brexit effect' on our politics: in the higher turnouts witnessed in both strongly Remain and Leave areas; in the drama of constituencies making hitherto inconceivable shifts across the political spectrum; in the final sweeping-away of the relationship between social class and party politics established in the post-war period; in the return to a two-party system seemingly so redolent of that era.

Brexit has become the issue *du jour*. It has dominated news coverage since the Referendum to a remarkable degree. It still dominates many a dinner-party debate (we hear). And, of course, Brexit was virtually all the Prime Minister spoke about as, on 18 April, she announced her doomed attempt to strengthen her position as Britain's Brexit leader.

And, as the negotiations over Britain's exit from the

European Union progress, there is little reason to believe that it will cease to shape our politics. Indeed, as these negotiations continue, and as the impact of leaving the European Union starts to become apparent, Brexit might – look away now if you are squeamish – come to dominate the political agenda even more than it already does.

Unsurprisingly for such a momentous event, the Referendum has already generated an outpouring of literary endeavours. From the self-justificatory (or self-exculpatory) memoirs penned by participants, to (occasionally) more sober and dispassionate analyses of the campaign written by observers, to the rare academic work that has appeared in what, for our profession, counts as a ridiculously short space of time,[3] the Brexit bookshelves are groaning already.

What the non-academic works in particular have in common is a narrow focus on a small cast of characters over a limited period of time. The decision to leave the European Union is explained in terms of the events between February and June 2016, events dominated by a few larger-than-life political figures. For these authors, all that happened on 23 June is explicable in terms of the often bitter and frequently bad-tempered interactions between the key public figures involved in the campaign itself.

To his credit, Tim Shipman – whose account of the Referendum is, in our opinion, one of the best, and certainly the most exhaustive – concedes that probably not all the answers can be found via such a narrow focus. As he puts it, there is 'a good case that four decades of euroscepticism, coupled with the Eurozone crisis and the mass migration from the Middle East, were more important than what happened in the campaign in determining the result'.[4]

We agree that the drivers of what happened are indeed long-term in nature. And, as we discuss in the chapters that follow, factors such as the Eurozone and migration crises clearly impacted on attitudes towards the European Union as the Referendum approached. We also argue, however, that Brexit cannot be explained simply in terms of these attitudes. The Referendum, and the events that have followed it, can only be understood via a grasp both of the UK's relationship with the EU and of more general developments in British politics over the last few decades. These include the broad convergence of the main political parties over matters ranging from the economy to a raft of 'values' issues; the consequent lack of mainstream political outlet for those outside this narrow consensus; increasing inequality and a lack of trust in political leaders; and a volatile electorate for whom parties no longer provided the kind of authoritative guidance they had at the time of the referendum of 1975.

None of these transformations concerned the EU *per se*, but they provided the context for a Referendum in which so many voted against the explicit advice of leaders, parties and experts. It is hard to underestimate the significance of a poll in which the majority of voters rejected the status quo in favour of an unknowable future.

And so our focus in this book is different from that adopted by most of the accounts published to date. This is not to say that the campaign was irrelevant, or that the roles of David Cameron, or Nigel Farage, or Boris Johnson were insignificant. Rather, our point is that the seeds of Britain's decision were sown over a far longer period.

Space constraints mean we must be selective about what we cover. There are some big issues that we cannot deal with in a short book like this. Most obviously, we leave aside questions concerning the future of the United Kingdom. As far as Scotland is concerned, the June General Election abated the risk of a second independence referendum, but we are not silly enough either to discount the eventual possibility or to try to predict its outcome. And the same goes for the question of how Northern Ireland's economy and, perhaps more importantly, its politics deal with the possible introduction of a 'hard' border between north and south. Nor do we have a great deal to say about the workings of the European Union itself. Brexit will doubtless impact upon the Union in myriad ways. We are not for a moment implying that these are neither interesting nor important, but they are not our focus.

In the final chapter, we consider how Brexit has already impacted upon our electoral politics and will continue to do so in months and years to come. Along the way, we express some opinions on what its impact on the country might be. But that is not our main concern. Those interested in what Brexit might mean in the years ahead could do worse than read the books by Ian Dunt and Daniel Hannan, which paint very different pictures of the UK's post-EU future.[5]

This slim volume is primarily about how the shifting nature of British politics and the long-term evolution of Britain's relations with the EU shaped the outcome of the Referendum, and what that outcome itself might mean for the future shape of our politics.

Preface

Our analysis will, we are sure, provide plenty of hostages to fortune. Many people are familiar with the conversation Chinese Premier Zhou Enlai had with Richard Nixon during the latter's visit to Beijing in 1972. When asked, so the story goes, about the impact of the French Revolution, the former is reported to have said it was 'too early to say'. It turns out, however, that the tale is in part apocryphal. It would appear that the Chinese Premier was referring not to the events of 1789, but to those of May 1968.

Nevertheless, Zhou was lucky. He had had a full four years to mull over the meaning of what had happened in that tumultuous year. We, in contrast, are writing about events going on around us. An election was called between when chapter 3 was finished and chapter 5 was started. Events had us reassessing our argument until the submission of the final manuscript. Partly because of this, we are deliberately cautious when it comes to the future, and all too well aware that even our timid forecasts may have proven misplaced before this book hits the shelves.

All that being said, we firmly believe that this is an important and necessary undertaking. For one thing, understanding the roots of what happened in June 2016 is crucial if we are to grasp what its implications could and should be. For another, however early it may be, it is important to try to untangle what is happening to politics in our country, albeit in the knowledge that others with more time to reflect on these events will, in due course, be able to produce more considered assessments.

Britain and its politics are changing. They will change still more as the Brexit process unfolds and the full implications of leaving the European Union begin to make themselves felt. We are living through one of those rare moments when an advanced liberal democracy might be witnessing a profound and far-reaching political recalibration. Its impact will be felt in all parts of our country, our economy and our society. This is our contribution to an understanding of that change and its origins.

A final word on sources and style. Unless otherwise stated, the evidence on public opinion we deploy is drawn from the numerous surveys conducted by the British Election Survey (BES). For stylistic reasons, we have used the terms 'United Kingdom' and 'Great Britain' interchangeably, and we apologize for any offence this may cause. And, finally, while on the subject of offence, we have, very occasionally, quoted people whose language leaves something to be desired. This was not with a view to shock, but rather to give a flavour of the febrile politics of the country at this time. Neither of us, be assured, ever swears.

1

The Best of Enemies

British relations with the various manifestations of European integration have never been comfortable. 'With Europe, but not of it', as Churchill put it, is probably the most upbeat assessment that could be made. Of all the member states, Britain has consistently been the least 'European' in its outlook, at the levels of both politics and public opinion.

The steady drumbeat of British euroscepticism, audible well before the United Kingdom joined the European Community, strengthened noticeably and possibly decisively after the signing of the Maastricht Treaty in 1992. This brought about a sea change in the nature of European integration, introducing the basis for the single currency as well as cooperation in areas such as defence policy and migration. Even prior to that, payments to the EU budget and the loss of sovereignty that EU membership implied had been long-standing bugbears, crucially joined, later in the day, by immigration. These discontents were given voice by a small but growing band of eurosceptics – both inside and outside parliament – whose rising influence was to prove decisive when it came to calling the 2016 Referendum.

This chapter pinpoints the factors that shaped British relations with the EU and explains how these ultimately led to a situation in which the UK voted to leave the Union. In tracing the history of relations between Britain and the EU, it shows how the themes that became so prominent in the Referendum campaign had in fact haunted the relationship for decades.

From then till (almost) now

The uncomfortable relationship between Britain and the institutions created by its European neighbours pre-dated formal membership. When the governments of France, West Germany, Italy, Belgium, Luxembourg and The Netherlands formed the European Coal and Steel Community (ECSC), Britain remained aloof. In 1957, the same six states established the European Economic Community (the EEC). Again, Britain was invited to participate. Again, it declined. By the early 1960s, economic growth in the six had begun to outstrip that of the UK. However, even once this led to London changing its mind, the experience was hardly salutory. Successive applications for membership from both Conservative and Labour governments were vetoed by French President Charles de Gaulle.

Nor did membership after 1973 lay British reservations to rest. Far from it. Whilst Labour had backed accession in 1967, by the time Britain joined six years later, it was politically expedient for the party to criticize the terms of entry. The 1974 Labour manifesto promised a fundamental renegotiation of the Treaty of Accession, which the newly elected Wilson government duly undertook. The ensuing talks achieved little of substance, but the resultant 1975 referendum produced an overwhelming vote in favour of continued membership. Even then, Britain remained wary of the club it had so recently joined. Immediately prior to the start of the 1977 British presidency of the EC, James Callaghan wrote to the General Secretary of the Labour Party emphasizing his concerns over the dangers of supranationalism and Britain's excessive budget contribution. Two years later, Margaret Thatcher entered Downing Street and immediately demanded that Britain's budgetary settlement be re-examined. In 1984, following years of belligerent rhetoric ('I want my money back') and bad-tempered bargaining, she secured a rebate on Britain's contributions to the Community budget. In 1988, the tone of her speech – at that altar of pro-European thought, the College of Europe in Bruges – caused consternation as she underlined her preference for cooperation among sovereign states, rather than control by supranational institutions.

That speech heralded the emergence of bitter divisions over Europe that have haunted the Conservative Party ever since. Labour, remember, had split into two parties in the 1980s partly because of disagreement over the EC, as key figures broke ranks to form the rival Social Democratic Party. Now, it was the turn of its opponents. Six Conservative Cabinet ministers resigned over Europe under Margaret Thatcher.

Mrs Thatcher's ultimate demise (itself prompted by struggles within her party over the EC) failed to resolve an issue that was coming to dominate British politics.

The UK now found itself almost alone among the member states in opposing further economic and political integration, and its recalcitrance greatly hampered the drafting of the Maastricht Treaty. The 1992 General Election reduced the Conservative majority in parliament from around 100 to just 21. Consequently, the government's policies towards the EU became the object of a ceaseless guerrilla war fought by Conservative eurosceptics enraged by the Treaty and energized by its (initial) rejection by a Danish referendum.

Maastricht represented a watershed moment. John Major, in fact, played a blinder at the summit. He secured amendments to, and opt-outs from, those things to which he objected – notably the Social Chapter, and Economic and Monetary Union, respectively. Nevertheless, the Treaty marked a shift in British relations with the EU.

To understand this, we need to step back a few years. In 1987, the EC member states had signed the Single European Act (SEA). This revision of the EC treaties led to the creation of the single market. And the UK had been one of the main driving forces behind this, as the Thatcher government was desperate to open up trade between the member states.

However, once the SEA was in place, the UK became, to all intents and purposes, a satisfied member state. As far as London was concerned, the single market was the final step in European integration. But this was not a belief shared by its European partners. The kind of talk the latter engaged in – of political or monetary union and other highly federalist sounding schemes – provoked nothing but incomprehension, mingled with concern, on the English side of the Channel. Hence the defensive and frequently belligerent reactions to each successive attempt to amend the EU treaties.

This reaction first became apparent during the negotiations over the Maastricht Treaty which was signed in 1992 – a year that also saw the entry into parliament of a new generation of Conservative politicians with a profound ideological hostility to European integration. Among them were some who were to play key roles in the 2016 Referendum (notably Iain Duncan Smith and Bernard Jenkin). Meanwhile, the Maastricht Treaty itself, with its plans for monetary union and common policies on migration and immigration, laid the groundwork for the key themes in the 2016 Referendum.

Compounding the impact of Maastricht, only a few months after the Treaty's signing, on what came to be known as Black Wednesday (16 September), Britain crashed out of the European Exchange Rate Mechanism (ERM). Despite spending billions of currency reserves and raising interest rates to a spine-tingling 15 per cent in an attempt to prop up sterling, the government proved unable to keep the pound above the lower limit set for it within the ERM.

The implications were far-reaching. For one thing, the humiliation dealt a fatal blow to the reputation of the Conservatives for sound economic management. Of more interest to us, it also impacted on attitudes to the EU, denting the notion that membership was good for the British economy. And this notion was to take another hit some twenty years later, as the Eurozone crisis ravaged the continental economy.

Finally, the Maastricht debates prompted the creation of a number of extra-parliamentary movements established specifically to call into question continued British membership of the EU. In 1991, a new party, the Anti-Federalist League, was created. This was followed in 1994 by the emergence of the Referendum Party, whose sole ambition was to press for a vote on EU membership. Having changed its name to the UK Independence Party, the former outlived the latter to become the one political party committed to ending membership. These extra-parliamentary forces created a 'pressure cooker' effect that played its part in radicalizing anti-EU sentiment *within* parliament.[1]

Following the Maastricht drama, Britain continued to act as a thorn in the side of its European partners. In 1994, Major vetoed the nomination of Jean-Luc Dehaene to succeed Jacques Delors as Commission President – only to see the job go to the equally federalist-leaning Jacques Santer. In retaliation to the EU's failure to lift a ban on the export of British beef following the BSE (or 'mad cow') scandal, he launched a policy of non-cooperation. Ministers and officials continued to attend EU meetings, but constantly raised the issue of beef exports while blocking anything requiring unanimous agreement – even if these had been British initiatives in the first place.

Following Major's defeat in 1997, his successor, Tony Blair, enjoyed a large parliamentary majority, and was far less hostile towards the EU than some of his Conservative predecessors. Policy under New Labour reflected this, though Chancellor Gordon Brown held his ground when Blair pushed to join the Euro. Despite the occasionally caustic tone with which British political leaders were wont to lecture their continental colleagues, and the bitterness that surrounded the Iraq War of 2003, relations with EU partners were not marked by the ill-tempered contestation of the Thatcher years.

That being said, the UK still proved a reluctant participant in negotiations over an EU constitution. When it came to signing the Lisbon Treaty that finally emerged in 2009, Brown, harried by domestic opponents of the Treaty, announced he was 'too busy' to attend, and a second ceremony had to be specially arranged for him. There was no little irony in the fact that it was the Conservative leader who had warned his party about the danger of 'banging on about Europe' who was to call the Referendum that made Europe a national obsession. David Cameron did so for a variety of reasons, largely connected with the poisonous split over the issue within his own party. Yet, to give him his due, he was forced to confront the issue at a perhaps uniquely difficult moment.

For one thing, the crisis in the Eurozone rumbled on throughout his tenure. The economic collapse of parts of the EU following the financial crisis of 2008 helped to undermine the notion (already called into question by Black Wednesday) that, for all its flaws, EU membership was positive for the British economy. Conservative eurosceptics complained loudly that the (relatively) healthy British economy was 'shackled to a corpse'. David Cameron's supposed 'veto' of the fiscal compact in December 2011 certainly played well to the Conservative Party gallery, but it also served to highlight the risks inherent in association with a struggling EU.

The Eurozone crisis had two other important consequences. First, it made London's position as the financial centre of the EU more uncomfortable. Other member states increasingly came to view it as the standard-bearer for the kind of unregulated capitalism that triggered the financial crisis in the first place.

Second, and more importantly, the economic travails

of the Eurozone led to a significant spike in migration from Eurozone states. Office for National Statistics (ONS) data illustrated that this began from the fourth quarter of 2012, as the divergence in growth between the UK and its Eurozone partners became manifest. The crisis thus turned the UK into a 'joint employer of last resort with Germany for a monetary union of which it was not a member'.[2]

Meanwhile, pressure began to build at home for a popular vote on EU membership. The willingness of politicians to duck their responsibilities by promising referendums on EU matters served to enshrine the legitimacy of the concept, while their repeated failure to deliver on their promises ramped up the pressure. Labour governments promised to consult the people both on joining the Euro and, in 2004, on the ratification of the European Constitutional Treaty. The following year, all three major parties promised the latter in their election manifestos. When Labour subsequently argued that the Lisbon Treaty that replaced the failed constitution did not warrant a referendum, Conservative leader David Cameron lambasted the decision as 'one of the most blatant breaches of trust in modern politics'. He then gave a 'cast-iron guarantee' to hold a popular vote on any text emerging from the Lisbon process. By November of the same year, he too had ruled out such a vote. By the time of the election in 2010, the Liberal Democrats were promising a referendum on membership. The following year, the Coalition government passed the European Union Act, which mandated that the people should have their say on any amendments to the EU treaties. Everyone, it seemed, thought referendums were a great idea.

Meanwhile, the political pressure on David Cameron

was mounting. In October 2011, the largest post-war parliamentary rebellion on Europe saw eighty-one Tories defy a three-line whip to back a referendum on EU membership (a mere forty-one had rebelled at the height of the Maastricht debacle). Vague promises about future referendums were not enough for a eurosceptic group whose suspicion of their leader had increased dramatically following his failure to act on his 'cast-iron' guarantee of a few years earlier.

Moreover, as the Conservative Party rebelled, the UKIP shadow lengthened. In the 2010 General Election, the party polled around 3 per cent – just 1 per cent more than they had done five years before. Yet, in 2009, it had come second in European Parliament elections with 16.5 per cent of the vote. By November 2012, it was finishing second in by-elections in Rotherham and Middlesbrough. By this time many believed that, if David Cameron failed to call a referendum, he could face a leadership challenge. In the month before he announced the Referendum, eleven of the twenty-seven polls carried out had UKIP ahead of the Liberal Democrats. Six of them had the Conservatives at less than 30 per cent.[3]

On 23 January 2013, David Cameron stood up in the offices of Bloomberg in London and announced that he would, if re-elected in 2015, seek to negotiate a 'new settlement' for Britain within the European Union and put the outcome to a Referendum on British EU membership. Rather than coming out in support of that membership, he made his support conditional on reforms along the lines he suggested.

The speech earned him a hero's welcome from his MPs. But it failed to shut the debate down. Ninety-five

Conservative backbench members of parliament signed a letter in January 2014 calling for parliament to be able to block EU laws via the repeal of the 1972 European Communities Act (tantamount to a rejection of membership). For the Conservative Party, Europe was becoming, as former Europe Minister David Lidington put it, 'like a Balrog waiting to be awakened'.[4] Unlike Gandalf, however, the Prime Minister was no wizard.

David Cameron's intervention at Bloomberg also failed to lance the UKIP boil. In 2014, the party won the European Parliament elections with 27.5 per cent of the vote (the first time in modern history that neither Labour nor the Conservatives won a national election). In August that same year, Conservative MP Douglas Carswell triggered a by-election in Clacton-on-Sea by defecting to UKIP. He cited a lack of faith in the willingness of the Prime Minister to secure meaningful concessions from the EU as his primary motivation. The following month, his colleague Mark Reckless also jumped ship. In the resultant by-elections, Carswell secured the biggest increase in vote share for any political party in any by-election when he recaptured his seat. The triumph of Reckless in Rochester and Strood on 20 November ramped up the pressure on the Prime Minister, and intensified speculation that more of his Conservative colleagues might be willing to defect to Nigel Farage's self-proclaimed 'insurrection'.

The Europe issue in British politics

So much for the story of British relations with the EU. These relations were rarely warm, and sometimes fraught. More specifically, however, they formed the context in which the British people were asked to vote on UK membership.

A number of key issues acted as constant irritants in Britain's relationship with the European club. And it is worth thinking about these briefly, if only because sovereignty (or 'control'), money and immigration were to be key themes in the 2016 Referendum campaign. The Leave campaign, in other words, did not conjure its arguments out of thin air.

Control

Many in Britain have long been suspicious of, or even downright hostile to, the power of and role played by the EU institutions. As early as 1962, Hugh Gaitskell had declared to the Labour Party conference that joining the EC would mean the 'end of a thousand years of history'. Picking up where he left off, in Bruges some twenty-five years later, Margaret Thatcher decried the centralizing tendencies of the EC, asserting that she had 'not successfully rolled back the frontiers of the state in Britain, only to see them re-imposed at a European level'. The *Sun* exemplified British concerns more pithily with its 'Up yours, Delors' headline of 1 November 1990.

During the bitter and protracted arguments over the Maastricht Treaty in the House of Commons, it was Tony Benn who, in November 1991, gave what Norman Tebbit described as the best speech he had ever heard in the House, lamenting that the Chamber 'has lost confidence in democracy. It believes that it must be governed by someone else.'

Angry debates over the Lisbon Treaty again revealed the

disquiet the supranational principle caused. Conservative commentator Peter Hitchens decried a treaty that would, as he put it, see 'beloved Britain' turned into 'a neglected outstation of the European Superstate, stripped of our nationhood, powerless to decide who lives here, controlled by laws we don't make and can't change, ruled by a government we cannot throw out'.

The issue of what came to be dubbed 'control' during the 2016 Referendum campaign, in other words, had haunted the UK's relationship with European integration from well before accession in 1973, and continued to do so thereafter. Irritated references to the 'unelected European Commission' were a staple of British political discourse. Warnings of the emergence of a European 'superstate' were commonplace. Meanwhile, eurosceptics fretted about the European Communities Act of 1972, which gave EU law primacy (or supremacy, in the jargon) over contradictory provisions in national law. The loss of sovereignty implied by membership, in short, was never fully accepted.

Money

Alongside such general concerns were more specific discontents with European integration. Prominent amongst these, for the duration of British membership, was money. A sense that the EU was a system somehow rigged against the UK has long been apparent in debates over the cost of membership, and, specifically, over contributions to the EU budget.

Nor was this wholly illusory. In discussions prior to British accession, the other member states had been careful to ensure that the newest member state paid generously for the privilege of joining. When it did so, it contributed 8.64 per cent of the budget, which had risen to 18.72 per cent in 1977. The whole edifice was contrived in such a way as to penalize those states that traded extensively outside the EU and that had relatively efficient agricultural sectors.

Arguments came to a head with the furious battles around Margaret Thatcher's demands to get 'her' money back. Even once she had secured the rebate, however, the contribution given to the EU remained a source of con siderable tension. Some two decades later, Tony Blair confronted Jacques Chirac at a 2005 European Council. After fifteen hours of talks, during which the two traded insults over Blair's 'pathetic' refusal to countenance renegotiation and Chirac's point blank rejection of any attempt to renegotiate the Common Agricultural Policy, German Chancellor Gerhard Schröder was moved to declare that the EU was 'in one of the worst political crises Europe has ever seen'.

Blair's decision to give up £1 billion a year of the rebate Mrs Thatcher had negotiated – almost one-third of the total – in return for a promise of future reviews of farm subsidies led to swift and almost universally critical domestic reactions. In a heated exchange, UKIP leader Nigel Farage accused Blair of being 'outplayed and outclassed at every turn' by Chirac. Shadow Foreign Secretary William Hague announced that Blair had given up £7 billion 'without securing anything in return'.

When budget negotiations came around again in 2013, David Cameron bragged he had battled off every attempt to change the rebate and could 'look taxpayers in the eye'. However – and indicative of the way in which political parties were willing to use the European issue as a stick to beat their opponents – the Labour

Party joined with Tory eurosceptics and voted against the government to pass an amendment calling for a real-terms cut in EU spending. Complaining loudly about the EU budget, and particularly about Britain's contribution to it, was simply good politics.

Immigration

Both sovereignty and money were longstanding issues that had created problems for the UK's relationship with its European partners since before formal membership of the EC. However, the single most crucial issue as the Referendum approached had become a source of concern far more recently. People's attitudes towards immigration were closely linked to their vote in the Referendum. Of those who believed there were too many immigrants in the UK, 51 per cent voted to leave the EU. In contrast, a mere 11 per cent of those who didn't share this concern supported Brexit. In the 1975 EU referendum, by contrast, the difference was far smaller (12 percentage points) and in the *opposite* direction.[5]

The catalyst for change was the decision to allow citizens of the states of Central and Eastern Europe unrestricted access to the UK following their entry into the EU. No other major 'destination country' in the EU followed this path. Indeed, all other EU member states except Ireland and Sweden applied some controls, notably a five-year transition period prior to opening borders – and labour markets – to nationals from the new member states. As a result, Britain received a historically unique inflow of migrants from the EU accession countries.

A key piece of evidence the government relied on when making its decision to allow unrestricted access was a Home Office report that concluded that net immigration from Central and Eastern Europe would be relatively small – between 5,000 and 13,000 immigrants per year.[6] In 2013, the ONS estimated the actual figure to be in the region of 50,000.[7] By 2014, there were nearly 1.5 million workers from Central and Eastern Europe living in the UK.[8]

The Home Office projection was based on the – as it turned out, incorrect – assumption that all fifteen EU countries would open their labour markets to the newcomers. Indeed, the authors of the report stated explicitly that, if Germany imposed transitional controls on free movement, around one in three of those who would have gone there might come to the UK. For what it's worth, this would have taken the prediction to 46,000 – pretty close to the eventual figure of 50,000 per year.

Whatever this says about the quality of the report itself, the fact is that the decision substantially changed the composition of immigration into the UK by displacing Commonwealth citizens as the largest source of foreign immigrants. The resultant – and unprecedented – inflow (for Britain and, specifically, for England) led to a growing link between public concern about immigration and negative attitudes towards the EU. And ultimately, of course, it was the public who were to get to decide the fate of EU membership.

What the people thought

For all the political interest in – not to say obsession with – European integration, and for all the increasing

15

scorn which the British media came to pour on 'Brussels' (particularly after the Maastricht debacle), public opinion did not, in general, share these preoccupations.

Ipsos MORI carries out regular surveys to find out what people think are the key issues facing the country. These reveal that the salience of the EU for the British public has been consistently low, despite brief – and generally modest – spikes in interest. Two such spikes occurred before the election of 1997 and in the period before May 2003, when the rumour took hold that Britain was preparing to adopt the single currency. In fact, the second-highest recorded level of interest – 40 per cent – would be reached only *after* the Referendum of 2016.

During the Maastricht debates, some Conservative rebels convinced themselves that the EU mattered deeply to the British public. But they were deluding themselves. The percentage of Britons citing Europe among 'the major issues facing Britain today' rose to double figures in the 1990s, reaching giddy highs of 20 and even 30% in the lead-up to the 1997 General Election and subsequently, but the EU never became a decisive political issue. Asked to choose from a list of things that were likely to determine their vote in April 1997, only 24% of respondents named the EU, compared to 62% citing education, 70% health, 50% law and order, and 45% unemployment.[9] In 2001, when William Hague tried in vain to rally voters around his EU agenda ('In Europe but not run by Europe') the figure stood at a mediocre 14% (as compared to 61% for the NHS), presaging a protracted fall in salience to single figures for over a decade, with only occasional flickers of interest.

Relative disinterest coexisted with limited support.

Immediately prior to the 1975 referendum, a Gallup poll had found that 41% would vote to leave the EEC; this dropped to 22% when people were then asked whether renegotiated terms of membership would alter their attitudes.[10] Whilst the referendum produced a vote to remain by roughly two-thirds to one-third, by March 1979 MORI found that 60% would vote to leave.

Following Prime Minister Thatcher's success in securing the budget rebate in 1984, and as the Labour Party began to move in a more pro-EC direction, opinion shifted. In 1987, the polls stood at 47% in favour of membership with 39% against. They reached their all-time high of 63% in favour versus 27% against in 1991 – just as the Conservative Party was busy tearing itself apart over the issue.[11] Throughout the 1990s, this trend was broadly maintained, albeit with dips brought about by periodic instances of tension between Britain and the EU – including John Major's policy of non-cooperation.

However, Eurobarometer polling since the 1990s revealed that just 30–40% of British citizens thought membership was a good thing – a lower percentage than in any other member state at any point over the past twenty years. Just as many were ambivalent, finding it neither good nor bad, and on average fully a quarter believed that it was a bad thing. This figure is not only well above the European average, it has been among the – if not *the* – highest of all member states in every year since the 1990s. The one exception was in 2011, when British antipathy was surpassed by a whisker – by that of the Greeks.

Moreover, the British have always had a noticeably weaker sense of Europeanness than people in other EU member states. An emphasis on a British rather than

European identity has held firm despite more than forty years of membership. Surveys conducted for the European Commission, for example, find that Britain is usually ranked 28 out of 28 in terms of its sense of European identity. Typically, nearly 60 per cent of Britons do not identify as European at all, compared to fewer than 40 per cent of the French, and only 30 per cent of Germans.[12] No other country, whether of the original six or the later accessions, matches this British sense of detachment.

British attitudes can thus be summarized in terms of general dislike combined with profound disinterest. The issue that changed this was the enlargement of 2004 and the decision of the British government not to impose limits on the rights of citizens of the new member states to come to the UK. Ipsos issue tracking revealed that public concern about immigration to Britain rocketed in the 2000s, as growing numbers of immigrants arrived in the UK.[13]

Figure 1.1 shows the increasing difference in EU approval scores between people who believe immigration is one of the most important issues facing the country, and those who don't.[14] In early 2004, there was a modest relationship between concern about immigration and disapproval of the EU. However, this strengthened significantly over time, with the EU approval gap between people who were concerned about levels of immigration and those who were not almost doubling by 2013.[15] In other words, within less than a decade of the 2004 enlargement, concern about immigration had gone from being moderately distinct from attitudes towards the EU, to being strongly associated with disapproval. And this was before the refugee

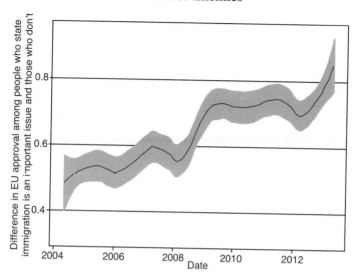

Figure 1.1 The EU and immigration

Source: Geoffrey Evans and Jonathan Mellon, http://whatukthinks. org/eu/immigration-and-euroscepticism-the-rising-storm.

of borders in the EU itself in 2015 placed the issue firmly in the headlines. It is not surprising, then, that, by 2015, support for leaving the EU was an astonishing 40 percentage points higher among those who believed that too many immigrants had been let in than among those who did not.

It's all in the timing

As the Referendum approached, pressure on the government was rising. And immigration had turned into a key issue – arguably *the* key issue – shaping attitudes towards the EU. Moreover, the broader context in which

19

this was happening was hardly encouraging. Contingent factors mattered, and one of those was timing.

As we've seen, it hardly helped the pro-EU cause that the Referendum coincided with the crisis in the Eurozone, not least as the economic rationale for membership had proven so persuasive over the years. Regular news coverage of the impact of austerity on Greece, coupled with talk of expensive bailouts, did little to reinforce this line of argument.

Nor did it help that the build-up to the Referendum coincided with the migration crisis that assailed southern Europe. Again, blanket news coverage played its part. And again, the UK was not directly affected. Non-membership of the Schengen border-free area insulated it from the worst effects, just as non-membership of the Euro did from EU-imposed austerity measures. However, it proved relatively easy for those committed to leaving to hint at the link between membership and the dangers of uncontrolled migration from the south.

Finally, sequencing, and particularly the proximity of a General Election to the Referendum, had important consequences. The pledge of the latter arguably helped David Cameron to secure victory in the former. Yet, equally, the steps taken to win the former undermined his ability to triumph in the latter.

As we've noted, the Prime Minister faced opposition both from UKIP and from within his own party in the run-up to the 2015 election. His response was to talk up what he could achieve from the renegotiation with the EU to which he had committed himself. And, of necessity, this applied to one area more than any other.

Migration was not even mentioned in the Bloomberg speech. However, confronted with the growing salience of the issue, the success of UKIP, and data illustrating that immigration was rising – despite Cameron's pledge to limit it to the 'tens of thousands' – the issue moved to centre stage. Addressing the Conservative Party conference in October 2014, he declared 'Britain, I know you want this sorted so I will go to Brussels, I will not take no for an answer and – when it comes to free movement – I will get what Britain needs.' Brave words indeed.

Tim Shipman details the angry fights that took place in the weeks between the Conservative Party conference and the major speech on immigration that Cameron planned to deliver in November. Whilst the Prime Minister and his staff favoured demanding some kind of emergency brake to allow the UK to stop admitting EU citizens under extreme circumstances, officials argued that this was impossible under EU law.[16]

At the last moment, the speech was amended and reference to the emergency brake removed in favour of a promise to limit access to in-work benefits, whilst preventing the payment of child benefit to children not in the UK. The retreat from a limit on numbers to one on eligibility for welfare was highly significant and would very much weaken the Prime Minister's hand when it came to the Referendum itself.

Despite this climb-down, however, the official tone remained belligerent and served to keep expectations high. The Prime Minister recognized in his much-anticipated immigration speech in November 2014 that people 'want government to have control over the numbers of people coming here'. As Shipman points out, this very language was to be appropriated by his opponents in the Referendum to come. As it was, the idea of limiting benefits rather than numbers found its way into the Conservative Party manifesto for the 2015 election, in the form of a four-year waiting period before EU migrants could claim.[17]

Perhaps these promises were intended merely as electoral sops, to be negotiated away during the formation of the coalition government most people expected to emerge from the election. Whatever the rationale, the Prime Minister had raised the stakes considerably ahead of negotiations with his EU partners.

Hold on to your buns

As we have seen, the campaign to leave the EU was a long time in the making. Anti-European arguments have long provided the 'background hum' of political discourse at Westminster and in the country in general. Indeed, the Leave campaign was effectively born in July 1993, when the Maastricht Treaty Bill was finally passed into law by the House of Commons.[18]

Sovereignty and the cost of membership had been bugbears for many years before David Cameron stood to make that fateful speech at Bloomberg. Immigration joined them as the 2000s progressed, and turned into the most toxic of issues as the Referendum approached.

Ultimately, the eurosceptic cause was significantly abetted by divisions inside the Conservative Party. Eurosceptic MPs were able to hold the government to ransom. And the Prime Minister had form when it came to caving in. In 2006, he sealed the Conservative leadership by promising to pull the party out of the European People's Party. In 2007, he gave a 'cast-iron' guarantee of a referendum on the Lisbon Treaty. In 2011, he wielded what he called his 'veto' of the Fiscal Compact Treaty. However, as former Conservative Chancellor Kenneth Clarke put it, 'If you want to go feeding crocodiles, then you'd better not run out of buns.' And bread proved to be in short supply.

Indeed, so attuned was the Prime Minister to the delicate sensitivities of the Tory right that he even resorted to rewriting history to placate them. His Bloomberg speech in many ways represented a reasoned enumeration of the benefits of EU membership. And, speaking of his desire for a new settlement, the Prime Minister added that 'When the referendum comes let me say now that if we can negotiate such an arrangement, I will campaign for it with all my heart and soul.' The phrase, considered offensive to some, was expunged from the transcript on the Number 10 website.

Yet Cameron's strategy of offering a Referendum at a moment when his own leadership was increasingly being questioned was initially successful. Two and a half years after his Bloomberg speech, he became the first full-term incumbent Prime Minister since 1832 to increase his party's share of the vote and total number of seats in the Commons.

However, the claims he had made as the election approached would come back to bite him.

2

Broken Politics

'Obviously I don't vote as I believe democracy is a pointless spectacle where we choose between two indistinguishable political parties, neither of whom represents the people.' We do not tend to regard Russell Brand as an authority on politics. That said, his comment contained more than a grain of truth about the state of British politics as the Referendum approached.

That Referendum marked the culmination not merely of a saga of strained relations between the UK and the EU, but also of processes that had progressively sapped faith and participation in British politics. A potent cocktail of factors – the growing similarity between the programmes and personnel of the main political parties, the shrinking role of elected government, and a succession of political and economic crises – conspired to undermine trust in politics and the major parties.

The explanation for this cannot be found in what social scientists call the 'demand-side'. In other words, the electorate itself can and should not be held solely responsible for falling political participation.[1] In fact, in many ways voters themselves have changed remarkably little: their preferences, their values, their concerns have remained relatively stable over time.

Rather, politics itself became detached from many of the people it was meant to represent and on whose participation it depended. Arguably, this mattered as much as attitudes towards the EU in shaping the outcome of the Referendum. It has also decisively shaped post-Referendum British politics.

Consensus politics

What became known as the post-war consensus (though it probably didn't feel like that at the time) came to an abrupt end following the 1973 oil crisis. Strikes, 3-day weeks, stagflation and the eventual intervention of the International Monetary Fund (IMF) revealed the weakness of the British economy and led to the polarizing politics of Thatcherism. The 1980s saw arguably the nearest thing to class war since the General Strike of 1926. Mrs Thatcher took on the National Union of Mineworkers, among many others. And the British economy was reshaped, moving away from manufacturing towards a greater reliance on the service sector.

The emergence of 'Blairism' in response to Labour's miserable showing during the 1980s has been well documented. So, too, has the journey the Labour Party consequently embarked upon towards the political centre ground. Highly symbolic steps, such as the dropping of Clause IV – the promise to nationalize industry that was seen as emblematic of the party's commitment to socialism – in 1995, and the removal of references to socialism in Labour manifestos, signalled a desire to leave class politics behind. This was made explicit in the 1997 manifesto:

> We aim to put behind us the bitter political struggles of left and right that have torn our country apart for too many decades. Many of these conflicts have no relevance whatsoever to the modern world – public versus private, bosses versus workers, middle class versus working class.

As Labour moved towards the ideological centre, the gap between the political programmes of the two major parties shrank.

Figure 2.1 summarizes the ideological location of the two major parties across a broad range of issues. The manifestos for each election are scored on a scale of 0 to 100 according to how left- or right-wing they are. High scores are right-wing.[2] It clearly illustrates the process of convergence that took place after the 1980s. By the 2000s, Labour, Conservatives and the Liberal Democrats were ideologically rather similar. This was

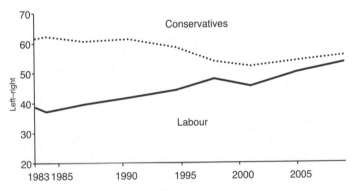

Figure 2.1 The converging positions of the parties' manifestos

Source: **Comparative Manifesto Project.**

not, it should be said, a purely British phenomenon. Across Western Europe as a whole, the distinction between the centre left and centre right became increasingly blurred.[3]

This growing 'elite consensus' was composed of several elements. In the first place – and perhaps most strikingly, given where it had come from (not to mention where it has arrived at the time of writing) – Labour embraced market-based economic policies. This was accompanied by a parallel rejection of state ownership, and indeed reluctance to countenance state intervention in the economy more generally. Second, there was broad if not unquestioning support for European integration – peaking in the early 2000s as the Blair government actively considered membership of the Euro. And finally, this consensus also included social as well as economic liberalism, especially when it came to issues such as gender equality and gay rights. In short, the Labour Party, like many other traditional social democratic parties, came to embrace the vision of a cosmopolitan, business-friendly technocracy.[4]

The adoption of a socially liberal agenda by both the main parties did not sit well with some sections of the electorate. And a focus on these issues shifted attention from the more traditional redistributive issues with which Labour in particular had been associated. When the fabulously wealthy Andrew Lloyd Webber flew back to the UK to vote in the House of Lords in favour of welfare cuts for the working poor – the previous time he voted was for gay marriage – Bridget Christie quipped that he 'loves gays but hates the poor'.[5] Harsh, no doubt, but with a nod towards the prevailing political *Zeitgeist*.

As the major parties became more ideologically alike,

they ended up competing over a set of issues located firmly in the political centre ground. The first victim was what used to be a defining feature of electoral politics – the advocacy of clear, competing political ideologies. Political competition came to be about little more than branding and competence, rather than policy substance.[6] Little surprise that the voters noticed. The phrase 'they're all the same' became an increasingly familiar criticism of politicians. Whereas in the 1980s, over 80 per cent of respondents thought there was a 'great deal of difference between the parties', since 1997 only around 25 per cent have thought so.[7]

The consequences of this political realignment were most keenly felt by one particular section of society. As it went about dropping references to 'socialism', Labour also abandoned talk of the group that had traditionally made up its core support – the working class. The party now targeted 'families' – preferably, of course, hard-working ones.[8]

The shift in policies was mirrored by an equally striking change in personnel. Half of the post-war Labour Cabinet had previously held working-class jobs. Former Conservative Chancellor and Home Secretary Kenneth Clarke described the Commons, at the time when he first entered it in 1970, as 'old landed gentry with rolling estates' on the one side, and 'retired trade union regional secretaries and 30-odd miners' on the other.[9] Yet when Labour entered office in 1997, there was just one Cabinet minister who had previously held a working-class job (John Prescott, later to be joined by Alan Johnson). Just as strikingly, between the 1950s and 1980s, around 10 per cent of Labour MPs had previously been union officials; by 2015, only 1 per cent had worked for a trade union.[10]

A similar story can be told when it comes to educational qualifications. In 1951, only 41 per cent of Labour MPs had been educated at university, compared with around 80 per cent by 2010. By the 1990s, the gap between Labour and Conservative MPs in university education had completely closed. In terms of educational background, social composition and substantive policy offerings, the two main parliamentary parties had become increasingly indistinguishable.

As a result, a gulf emerged between the major parties and those voters who were not university educated and middle class. And this mattered, because the background of politicians has been shown to influence the sorts of policy positions they advocate.[11] Moreover, voters tend to trust those politicians to whom they can most easily relate. A recent experimental study, for example, found that working-class people are more negative about wealthy political candidates, particularly when it comes to their perceived 'approachability'.[12]

Little wonder, then, that, as the parties converged, so too voters' perceptions of whom they represented also changed. By 2001, the proportion of voters who felt that Labour represented the interests of the working class had dropped from 47% (in 1987) to 10%. By 2015, 88% said that the Conservatives were a middle-class party, but only 38% thought that Labour was a working-class party. In fact, more people (48%) thought that Labour too was a middle-class party.

Britain's party system, in other words, came to be dominated by two solidly centrist and liberal, middle-class parties. At the same time, mainstream party politics became professionalized, a niche activity that attracted the highly educated with the contacts, resources and skills to join the think tanks, network with the right people, and climb the greasy political pole: a political class removed from many – on both left and right – whom it was meant to represent.

Anti-politics

As political parties have changed, so, too, has what politicians aspire to do in government. We've already mentioned how the narrowing of the ideological gap between centre left and centre right reduced political competition to increasingly dry contests over credibility and competence. Technical competence, in other words, replaced ideology as the crucial battleground.

Yet with politics becoming more technical, so too have ever more key public policy responsibilities been handed over to non-political bodies. From central banks to regulatory agencies, public policy is increasingly made 'at arm's length' from politicians.

Whilst some were offended to hear (independent) Bank of England Governor Mark Carney assert, in October 2016, that that Bank was 'not going to take instruction on our policies from the political side', he was in fact merely stating a fact. Indeed, almost ten years earlier, Alan S. Blinder, former Deputy Chair of the US Federal Reserve, had suggested that the model of independence applied to central banks should be extended to other areas such as health and welfare, with elected politicians making way for unelected experts.[13]

He was far from alone. Numerous academics have argued that such 'delegation' by politicians provides a more effective means of making long-term decisions than policy making by elected politicians. And as far as some technocrats are concerned, democracy is 'simply incompatible with the realities of a complex post-industrial society'.[14]

There are even those for whom shifting responsibility away from politicians is a way to enhance democracy. Lord Falconer proclaimed enthusiastically that the 'depoliticisation of key decision-making is a vital element in bringing power closer to the people'.[15] The people he meant, presumably, being bankers and regulators. The problem with all this, of course, is that depoliticization has contributed towards reducing interest in, and engagement with, democratic politics, as more and more of the levers of power slip from the grasp of those the public elect.

A further consequence is that policy debates came to be couched in increasingly impenetrable jargon. New Labour bears a disproportionate share of the blame for the emergence of 'governance by gobbledegook'. And this frequently implied governance by euphemism. Terms such as 'structural adjustment' or 'downsizing' were coined to avoid more inflammatory – and comprehensible – alternatives such as 'reducing wages' or 'sacking people'.

Such trends alone might have been expected to have turned voters off, but they were reinforced by others that have limited the scope of democratic politics still further. For while policy making at home has been increasingly farmed out to technocrats and experts, these tendencies have been reinforced from outside.

Globalization is routinely held up by political leaders as representing a constraint that limits their policy options. As Tony Blair memorably put it to the 2005

Labour Party conference, 'I hear people say we have to stop and debate globalization. You might as well debate whether autumn should follow summer.' The analogy is, of course, profoundly misleading. Globalization is the product of decisions taken by politicians and not the kind of unchallengeable constraint it is often portrayed as being. Yet as long as it is seen – or at least depicted – as such by politicians, their room for political manoeuvre decreases.[16] As the 'imperatives' of globalization closed off policies that challenged the prevailing status quo (which, as we've seen, the domestic elite consensus largely bought into), so too did the relevance of politics to those outside the ideological mainstream decline.

The European Union itself forms part of this picture. If the constraints imposed by globalization are frequently exaggerated, those implied by EU membership are real enough. Whilst the most egregious example of this is the enormous influence of the Union over the economic policies of Eurozone members, it extends further. EU law restricts what member states are able to do. Whilst much of the rhetoric around EU regulations and their impact has been misleading and exaggerated, these rules do, nonetheless, act as a constraint – witness the frustration of Conservative MPs, referred to in the preceding chapter, concerning the principle of the supremacy of EC over national law.

There are three further ways in which European integration can impact on national democracy. First, by constraining policy choices, it limits competition between political parties. Second, and for similar reasons, it limits the repertoire of national governments. Third, and more speculatively, it is possible that a lack of respect for, and interest in, members of the European Parliament, along with habits of not voting in European elections, might have spilled over into attitudes and behaviours at the national level.[17]

The combination of broad convergence between the major parties, the trend towards delegation of key functions to non-elected bodies, and the constraints imposed by globalization and the EU fostered the impression that political leaders could achieve less and less. This was the era of TINA ('there is no alternative') politics. Little wonder that participation in democratic politics came to seem less important.

Detachment and disinterest

As politics changed, so too popular interest in it declined. That a major British newspaper could herald a turnout of 72.2% in the 2016 Referendum as 'huge' underlined the extent to which we have become accustomed to low levels of political participation in elections more generally.[18] In the 1970s and 1980s, close to 80% would go to the polls. Between 1992 and Blair's 'New Labour' landslide in 1997, turnout dropped from 77.7% to 71.4%. Since the turn of the century, prior to the Referendum, the average has been around 63%.

This decline can be attributed in part to the restricted choices offered by the parties. If it doesn't make much difference which way you vote, and – worse still – none of the parties offer the policies you believe in, why make the effort? A survey of non-voters by Survation found that the overriding reasons for abstention were a sense of not being represented by candidates, that voting made no difference, and that all candidates were the same.[19] Similarly, the *British Social Attitudes Report* found in 2015 that around one quarter of the British population believed that 'it's not really worth voting'.[20]

As turnout declined, we also witnessed a striking fall in party membership. Combined Labour and Conservative Party membership stood at 3.4 million in 1964. By 2013 (prior to the recent surge in Labour membership generated by the Corbyn leadership campaign), Labour had 190,000 members, the Conservatives 150,000.

This in turn was accompanied by a marked fall in levels of identification with the major parties. Back in the 1960s, nearly half of the electorate identified strongly with a political party. By 2005, this figure had fallen to 10%. While it has increased a little in recent years to 15%, this has been more to do with the arrival of new choices via parties such as UKIP than with renewed attachment to the older ones.[21]

The loosening of the connections between parties and voters has helped to generate what is known as political volatility. As voters become less attached to individual parties, they become less consistent in their political preferences. If the parties become more alike, there's less reason to stick loyally with one or the other. The 2010–15 electoral cycle witnessed the highest recorded levels of individual-level vote change, the culmination of a fifty-year trend. In the 1960s, around 10% of people changed their vote from one election to another. In 2015, almost 40% did so.[22] Pity the pollsters.

As we might expect, this disconnection from politics hasn't affected all parts of society equally. Turnout used to be similar across all classes and education groups. In 1987 and 1992, for example, less than 5 percentage points separated turnout by people with little education from that by the more highly educated. The same small difference separated the middle class and working class back in the 1960s and 1970s. By 2015, however, estimates suggest that over 85% of the middle class and educated voted, compared to a mere 48% of those with a working-class job and little education.[23] Similarly, turnout amongst the poorest income quintile had only been 4% lower than that of the wealthiest in 1987, but by 2010 this gap had reached 25%.[24]

In short, the working class, the poor and the less highly educated, on both left and right, increasingly came to feel that none of the mainstream parties represented them, and accordingly chose not to vote at all. Little wonder the Institute for Public Policy Research described the UK as a 'divided democracy'.[25]

Dysfunctional politics

More recent events served merely to compound this situation. In May 2009, the *Daily Telegraph* began publishing details of the expenses claims made by MPs. Three members of the House of Commons and one peer were subsequently jailed, while blanket coverage in the media, not to mention the egregious nature of some of what was uncovered – claims for floating duck islands, moats and paid-off mortgages were amongst the highlights – both played their part in shaping public perceptions.

Soon after the *Telegraph* began to chronicle the scandal, Ipsos MORI found a spike in negative attitudes towards the workings of government.[26] Meanwhile, an

ONS report of November 2010 revealed a halving in levels of trust in political parties. A mere 9% of adults at this point were willing to admit to trusting political parties, compared to 18% a year earlier. The *British Social Attitudes Report* of December 2010 found that 4 in 10 people no longer trusted politicians to put the national interest first, while the majority of voters believed MPs never told the truth. On this measure, mistrust in politics was now four times higher than in the mid-1980s and more recent BSA surveys indicate it has not since returned to anywhere near that earlier level.[27]

Depressingly, insofar as the crisis did not have any marked long-term impact, this was largely because levels of confidence in politics were already so low. Net trust ratings for parliament at the end of 2009 were –47%. In other words, they were already so low that they could not really decline any further – what is known in social science as a 'floor effect'.

There was more to come. The expenses scandal broke at a time of rising economic inequality. In 1980, the top 10% earned 2.7 times as much as the bottom 10%; by 2013, this figure had risen to 3.7. As far back as 2000, the share of working-age men without qualifications who were not active in the labour force had reached 30%, compared to less than 4% two decades earlier. By April 2016, that figure stood at over 43%.[28]

Inequality was compounded by the policies put in place by the Coalition government in response to the financial crisis. Austerity was estimated by the Institute for Fiscal Studies (IFS) to have cost each household £1,127 a year. Inevitably, the impact varied across society. In 2015, the IFS concluded that it was low-income families with children that had borne the brunt of the

Coalition's austerity drive. In contrast, middle- and higher-income households had escaped 'remarkably unscathed' from tax and benefit changes.[29]

By February 2014, almost twice as many voters as when the Coalition had come to power in May 2010 felt worse off financially, and this despite a series of positive economic growth forecasts and falling unemployment. As we shall see in the following chapters, the gap between official figures and people's experience was to prove important during the Referendum campaign. It was only in February 2016 that the Resolution Foundation concluded that living standards in the UK had finally made up the ground lost as a result of the financial crash.

Alongside the unequal impact of austerity policies themselves, the government contributed to undermining its oft-repeated claim that the British people were 'all in this together'. In January 2012, the Prime Minister failed to block RBS Chief Executive Stephen Hester's £1 million bonus. At the same time, the bank, under pressure from the government, was announcing a further 4,450 job losses (bringing the total to 34,000 since 2008). Three years earlier, Cameron himself had argued against bonuses for banks that were majority-owned by the taxpayer, on the grounds that people 'who work hard and have paid their taxes are seeing billions of pounds of taxes go into these banks and yet large bonuses are still being paid. That's just wrong.' The Chancellor's decision to cut the 50p top rate of income tax and freeze personal allowances for pensioners in the Spring 'Billionaire's Budget' further undermined the idea that austerity was being implemented fairly.

Such public policy missteps were matched by a series

of more personal misjudgements. First came George Osborne's 'great train snobbery'. Caught in first-class with a standard ticket, Osborne and his entourage were accused of trying to avoid paying the upgrade by insisting that there was no alternative seating arrangement befitting the minister. In October, government Chief Whip Andrew Mitchell was accused of calling a policeman a 'pleb' for challenging his right to enter Downing Street, sparking a tsunami of criticism of the 'posh boys' running the country.

All of this had a profound impact on public attitudes. A YouGov poll in 2014 suggested there had clearly been a negative shift in the way the public viewed politicians. It found that 48% now believed that politicians were 'out for themselves', with a further 30% believing they were out for their party, and just 10% thinking they wanted to do what was right for the country.[30] By 2015, 75% of working-class people believed it was difficult to move between classes – an increase of over 10% since the recession.[31] This merely reinforced the resentment felt by those 'left behind' with a political system that did not seem to work for them.

As early as 2011, David Cameron's pollster, Andrew Cooper, was warning colleagues that people were coming to the conclusion that the Conservatives were not on their side, adding that the phrase 'we're all in this together' – which had initially polled positively – now merely elicited laughter.

Labour fared little better. For all that Ed Miliband's manifesto of 2015 revealed an appreciation of the problems that many people faced, his campaign failed to convince – or even get through to – enough voters. While Labour performed slightly better than the Conservatives in polling around the impact of austerity, the reputation of established political parties as a whole suffered. By March 2015, 60% of those asked felt Labour had 'seriously lost touch with ordinary working people'.[32]

The populist alternative

The widening gap between politicians and the people provided fertile ground for parties that defined themselves in opposition to the political consensus. Populism has been defined as an ideology that 'separates society into two homogeneous and antagonistic groups' – ordinary people and a corrupt elite – and that believes that politics should be an expression of the 'will of the people'.[33] Prevailing dissatisfaction with, and distrust of, mainstream politics represents a powerful recruiting tool for such movements.[34]

They certainly helped fuel the drift of voters towards UKIP. The party's voters are steadfastly negative about the political class. Some 74% believe that politicians are out for themselves (versus 48% amongst voters as a whole), with a paltry 3% (versus 10%) thinking they are out to do their best for their country. This belief that politicians are largely self-serving is a distinctive feature of UKIP supporters, who hold unambiguously and intensely negative views of mainstream politics and politicians.[35]

The expenses scandal played its part here. Former Conservative Party Chairman Lord Tebbit advised people not to vote for candidates from the major parties, who had behaved like 'welfare junkies', in the European elections of 2014. His comments were widely assumed to represent an endorsement of UKIP.[36] Opinion polling in May 2009 had shown that support for fringe parties had jumped by some 9% since April.[37]

The lingering impact of the financial crisis also played its part. Research has revealed that financial crises tend to lead to increased political polarization as policy uncertainty rises and government majorities shrink. And it is the far right that tends to profit because of its tendency to blame foreigners or minorities. A study of twenty advanced economies over more than 140 years suggests that, in the five years following a systemic financial crisis, these parties have benefitted, on average, from a 30% increase in vote share, compared to pre-crisis levels.[38]

But the populist story is not simply one about the financial crisis, inequality and tone-deaf politicians. It is also about social values. These involve issues such as respect for traditional values and attitudes towards crime and punishment, censorship and authority.

The spectrum from socially conservative to socially liberal values is quite distinct from the traditional left–right divide that has dominated our politics. When it comes to these values, it is not merely those in low-skill jobs, or with no jobs, who have felt unrepresented by mainstream socially liberal parties. Social conservativism has a wide social base, encompassing many occupations and social classes. It includes the self-employed, small business owners and a substantial proportion of managers.

The disconnect between the views of the main parties and those of large numbers of the electorate on social values can be seen, for example, with regard to the death penalty. Abolition of the death penalty was passed in parliament in the 1960s by an overwhelming majority of MPs. Yet public opinion was strongly opposed to abolition. Even in the 1970s, more than three-quarters of the population supported the death penalty. While there has been a gradual erosion in support, the latest BSA report still shows that support for the death penalty (45%) still leads opposition to it (37%) by 8 percentage points (16% are unsure where they stand).[39] A recent BBC poll found that even voters aged 18–21 were only fractionally less likely to support capital punishment for serious crimes (56%) than the population as a whole (59%).[40]

Other opinions that tap into social values, for example regarding the role of women in society and the workplace, or attitudes towards homosexuality or minorities and immigration, reveal marked differences between younger and older generations, and between people with or without higher educational qualifications. Only the former in each case hold liberal positions similar to those typically advocated by the established parties.

UKIP certainly capitalized on growing dissatisfaction with politics, on frustration born out of the impact of the financial crisis, and on the growing disconnect between the major parties and many voters when it came to social values. And, of course, it capitalized on one issue more than any other. As early as 2005, the party's manifesto declared that current levels of immigration resulting from deliberate government policy and the Eastern enlargement of the EU were unsustainable. And its support, as we have seen, increased steadily towards the end of the decade.

This was not because voters had become more intolerant or hostile towards immigrants. Indeed, anti-immigrant attitudes have, if anything, decreased over the long term (as can be seen in figure 2.2).

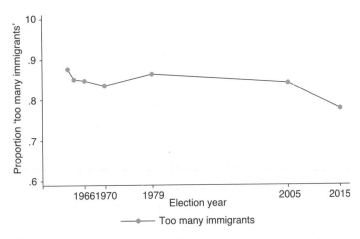

Figure 2.2 '*Do you think that too many immigrants have been let into this country?*'

Source: BES.

Nonetheless, as figure 2.2 also shows, there has always been a sizeable bloc of voters – around 80% – who think immigration is too high and who could, perhaps, be mobilized politically if the issue became salient. UKIP simply adopted a 'fusion' strategy, connecting the issues of immigration and EU membership – which, as we saw in chapter 1, voters were already starting to do themselves following the 2004 EU expansion – and to good effect.[41]

By the local elections of 2013, UKIP averaged almost 25% of the vote – an increase of almost 10% from four years earlier. Its national equivalent vote share increased from less than 5% to almost 20%. A year later, when the party won the European elections, immigration was again front and centre in its campaign. Nigel Farage argued that mass migration was making parts of the country 'unrecognisable' and 'like a foreign land', while putting pressure on schools and hospitals.[42] What's more, people were starting to believe that UKIP might just do something to change this. The Conservative-led government had made a lot of noise about drastically reducing net immigration to the tens of thousands annually, but consistently failed to deliver even a modest fall. This didn't go unnoticed. In 2015, the BES found that 42% of people thought the Conservatives would try to reduce immigration if they got in, but only 19% thought they would succeed. Comparable figures for UKIP, given their stated policy of leaving the EU, were 81% and 56%. The Leave campaign was gathering momentum.

The bottom line

This chapter has painted a stark picture of the state of British politics as the Referendum approached. By the time of its eighth annual *Audit of Political Engagement* in 2012, the Hansard Society had uncovered what it said was a 'disturbing' new trend. Indifference to politics, it argued, was hardening into 'something more significant', with interest, knowledge, satisfaction and engagement falling, at times sharply.[43] The number of people certain not to vote increased to its highest-ever mark.[44] The report for the following year concluded that this was no 'temporary blip', suggesting that 'a more severe form of disengagement than anything previously seen during the Audit lifecycle is now setting in'.[45]

For their part, the authors of the 2010 *British Social Attitudes Report* argued that, while confidence in the political system had never been particularly high, the expenses scandal appeared to have 'eroded trust yet further'. Their conclusion was stark. The survey 'might lead one to suggest that a public that has long had its doubts about the trustworthiness of its political class is now on the verge of being straightforwardly cynical in its attitude towards government and politicians'. Little wonder that the doyen of the study of political parties, Peter Mair, was moved to remark that the age of party democracy had passed.[46] By 2016, MORI's Veracity Index had politicians coming last in a list of trusted professions (24th out of 24). To add insult to injury, government ministers came in at 23.

Public attitudes stemmed partly from short-term factors – the expenses scandal, the financial crisis and the austerity policies subsequently pursued. They were also, however, the result of longer-term trends. In the two decades prior to the EU Referendum, Britain's major political parties coalesced around a centrist, socially liberal, pro-European consensus, which – combined with the country's 'first past the post' voting system – provided little obvious outlet for the socially conservative preferences of many voters. Among a large proportion of these people, as we saw in the last chapter, euroscepticism took on additional resonance as the European Union became associated with unprecedentedly high levels of immigration.

Clearly, the policies favoured by New Labour and the Conservatives were not identical. New Labour in power pursued a redistributive agenda that helped to transform many lives. But it was social democracy by stealth, social democracy implemented surreptitiously so as not to offend the centrist voters and businesses whose trust the party sought. The Conservatives, as we have seen, pursued a very different economic agenda. But they too moved to the centre, with their adoption of socially liberal policies on gender, race and sexual orientation. The perception among many was that the two had become indistinguishable.

An increasingly disenchanted electorate was thus confronted with a limited set of political choices. And this created a climate for rebellion.

3

The Referendum

The 2015 Conservative victory paved the way for the EU Referendum. This duly took place a little over a year later. Our aim here is not to rehash the history of the campaigns. There are plenty of places to go for blow-by-blow accounts of the intrigue, plotting and breath-taking amounts of swearing that formed the backdrop to the vote.

Rather, what we're looking to do here is to identify the key themes of the campaign, and particularly the ways they built on those identified in previous chapters. In this sense, the chapter acts as a bridge between our analysis of the longer-term factors that drove the Referendum outcome, and the impact that the process has exercised, and will continue to exercise, on British politics.

To this end, after briefly reviewing the course of the campaign, we look in more detail at the arguments presented by the Leave camp, which were to prove so influential both before and after the Referendum. We then consider the nature of the Referendum debate and of the competing claims advanced by both sides. Finally, we turn to the relationship between the debate over Brexit and a party system that struggled to contain it.

Dave's deal

It is easy enough to understand why David Cameron decided to embark on a renegotiation prior to holding a Referendum on EU membership. British Social Attitudes data from 2015 revealed that 37 per cent of respondents favoured reducing the powers of the EU and remaining inside, as compared with 26 per cent in favour of maintaining the then-current relationship, and only 18 per cent in favour of leaving. A significant majority of voters, in other words, were willing to remain within a reformed EU.

The problem, however, lay in the Prime Minister's ability to sell whatever he achieved as a genuine and meaningful 'reform'. As we have seen, he himself had raised expectations in the run-up to the General Election. He raised them still further via a report in the *Daily Telegraph* on 5 December which claimed he would lead the 'Out' campaign if the renegotiation were unsuccessful. Any deal would thus have to deliver enough to justify, convincingly, his leaving his much-trumpeted euroscepticism behind him and campaigning for continued membership.

The renegotiation also meant that Cameron was not able to campaign immediately. For 3 of the 3½ years between the Bloomberg speech and the Referendum itself, the pending renegotiation meant that he could not publicly make the case for continued EU membership. Paul Stephenson, Communications Director for Vote Leave, commented that, far from 'rolling the pitch' – as Conservative strategists dubbed their tactics in the run-up to political campaigns – the renegotiation was more akin to scuffing it up.[1]

Ironically enough, the renegotiation itself proceeded remarkably smoothly. Indeed, long before the commencement of formal talks, the EU had already embraced much of the Prime Minister's competitiveness agenda, with the withdrawal of almost 300 legislative proposals. Moreover, the conclusions of the European Council meeting of 26–27 June 2014 went a significant way towards addressing his concerns regarding the notion of 'ever closer union'.[2]

Nor did Cameron come away from the crucial summit of 18 and 19 February 2016 empty-handed. A single member state was hardly going to be able to bring about a fundamental transformation of the EU, particularly when formal changes to the Treaty were simply not on the cards. Indeed, it is hard to conceive of circumstances in which the requisite unanimity for Treaty change could be achieved between member states in the foreseeable future.

All this being said, the Prime Minister managed to extract important concessions. He secured a British exemption from the idea of 'ever closer union', to be written into the treaties at a future date. He negotiated a guarantee that non-Euro states would not fund Euro bailouts, and would be reimbursed for any central EU funds used to prop up the currency. A new procedure meant that legislative proposals by the Commission could be blocked by 55 per cent of the EU's national parliaments. And on free movement, Cameron not only won the ability to restrict payments of in-work benefits and child support, but also secured provision for what could be seen as an emergency brake on migrant numbers in the case of overriding reasons of public interest.

One can argue about whether or not these changes would have had much in the way of practical value. Economists, for instance, insisted that the changes to migrant worker benefits would have little or no impact on the number of EU citizens coming to the UK. However, this is to miss the point – for the renegotiation was, at heart, a political and public relations exercise.

Judged in these terms, the outcome was less than positive. The renegotiation did not produce the whole-sale new settlement the Prime Minister had spoken of. Assurances of future Treaty amendments to enshrine the opt-out from ever closer union were not the same as the 'full-on treaty change' Cameron had once promised. In areas such as financial services and social and employment legislation, where the Conservative Fresh Start Group had long called for action, nothing was done. The pledges from the Conservative Party manifesto to restrict the ability to send child benefit abroad and to make workers from other member states ineligible for welfare payments were not kept, or at least not in their entirety. And, crucially, it proved difficult to come up with a straightforward solution to the problem of the numbers of EU citizens entering the country.

The Prime Minister's own party was quick to express its disapproval. On 2 February 2016, following publication of a draft agreement between the Prime Minister and Donald Tusk, President of the European Council, the normally soft-spoken Conservative MP Steve Baker rose in the House of Commons to declare that:

This in-at-all-costs deal looks funny, it smells funny, it might be superficially shiny on the outside but poke it and it's soft in the middle. Will my right Honourable

Friend admit to the House that he has been reduced to polishing poo?

A survey carried out between November and December 2015 had found a high proportion of Tory MPs waiting on the outcome of the renegotiation before deciding how to vote in the Referendum.[3] In the weeks leading up to the crucial EU summit at which the deal was to be agreed, civil servants were confidently predicting that only 'around 40 or 50' would defect and throw their support behind Brexit. In the event, over 140 ultimately did so. A follow-up poll a year later underlined that more than half of those who eventually backed Leave had adopted that stance following the renegotiation.[4]

The outcome of the renegotiation mattered enormously. Private polling carried out by Downing Street had showed that, if Cameron had come back with a deal supported by Boris Johnson and other senior Tories, a significant number of Conservative voters would have backed him.[5] Politicians provide important cues to public opinion. The high number of Tory defectors, and the presence among them of popular figures such as Johnson and Michael Gove, no doubt emboldened Conservative voters to defy their Prime Minister and vote for Brexit.

The relative lack of political support was as nothing compared to the outraged reaction of the eurosceptic press. 'Call that a deal, Dave?' bellowed the *Daily Mail*. Perhaps more disappointingly and certainly more surprisingly for the Number 10 team, *The Times* was also roundly critical of the 'fudge' the Prime Minister had achieved. Some weeks later, Cameron himself was reportedly moved to a 'red-faced four-letter rage' on hearing the *Sun* was planning to back Brexit.[6]

Having argued against the status quo, the Prime Minister ultimately got a deal that, to most observers, did not seem fundamentally to change it. The perception of failure was merely reinforced by the Remain camp's decision to avoid all mention of the renegotiation once the campaign proper had kicked off.

The campaign

The campaign began in earnest once the Prime Minister had returned from Brussels and announced his intention to hold a Referendum on 23 June.

The Remain camp deliberately attempted to win the economic argument early. A mere 24 hours after the Prime Minister's statement, the CEOs of a third of the FTSE 100 companies signed a letter in *The Times* arguing against Brexit. Over subsequent weeks, the campaign maintained a steady barrage of information about the economic damage that leaving the EU would inflict upon the country. By mid-April, most observers agreed that the economic argument had been won.

Victory, however, meant that the media were keen to shift on to other issues. Lord Mandelson reports one journalist saying to him: '[Y]ou've won the economic argument hands down, so we can move on.'[7] The contrast with the Scottish referendum is instructive here. During that campaign, the economic arguments against independence were presented only a few weeks before the actual vote, serving to maximize their impact.

During the early stages of the campaign, Britain

Stronger in Europe also profited from being able to draw upon the full weight of the British state. The civil service proved an invaluable resource. On 6 April, a booklet was sent to every home in the country setting out the (primarily economic) case for remaining in the EU. Twelve days later, the Treasury published a study warning of the dire economic costs of Brexit.

At the end of May, however, the rules of the game changed. The start of the so-called 'purdah' period meant that government departments were prohibited from engaging in activity that could be seen as an attempt to influence the outcome. It also meant that the media had to give more time to the Leave side. At the same time (and not coincidentally), the latter was changing its message.

In the initial stages of the campaign, Vote Leave had deliberately attempted to differentiate itself from the UKIP-dominated Leave.EU. The reason was neatly summarized by Sunder Katwala as the 'Farage paradox'. In a nutshell, the higher UKIP's media profile, poll rating and membership rose, the more support for leaving the EU shrank. Whilst Nigel Farage acted as a magnet for confirmed eurosceptics, he put off undecideds because of what Douglas Carswell was fond of describing as his 'angry nativism'.[8]

To distinguish themselves, Vote Leave initially chose to highlight issues other than immigration. Michael Gove's 'coming out' in the pages of the *Spectator*, published on 20 February 2016, focused exclusively on democratic control, the money paid to Brussels, and the fact that the United Kingdom would be 'freer, fairer and better off outside the EU'.[9] This focus was maintained for the first couple of months of the campaign.

Following a faltering performance and a series of apparent gaffes in March, however, it was revisited. The focus of the campaign gradually began to shift. On 26 May, the ONS published figures revealing that net migration in 2015 had been 333,000 – the second-highest figure on record. Dominic Cummings, Campaign Director for Vote Leave, declared to Johnson and Gove that if 'you want to win this, you have to hit Cameron and Osborne over the head with a baseball bat with immigration written on it'.[10]

The day after the figures were released, purdah began. The Leave campaign chose this moment to unveil a series of policy initiatives. On 15 June, they announced that, in the event of a vote for Brexit, they would repeal the European Communities Act, pass legislation guaranteeing some of the savings from membership to the NHS, and end the supremacy of the European Union's Court. Where the campaign got the authority to issue policy pledges from was anyone's guess. Nonetheless, they had the effect of shifting the debate to the opportunities that Brexit would supposedly provide.

Most importantly, the pledges included one on the adoption of an Australian-style points-based system, with the stated intention of controlling immigration. Boris Johnson and Michael Gove both stressed that Brexit was the only way to reassert control over the country's borders. Johnson predicted that the population would rise 'to about 70 million or perhaps 80 million' if free movement continued unchecked. In a joint letter to the Prime Minister, they argued that the government's commitment to limit migration to the tens of thousands was unachievable as long as the UK remained in the EU.

Turkey, too, became an issue. Armed Forces Minister

Penny Mordaunt went on *The Andrew Marr Show* to argue that the UK could not stop it from joining the EU. Gove, for his part, claimed that Turkey and four other countries could join by 2020, leading to over 5 million people coming to the UK. The new tactics had an immediate impact. In the fourteen polls between 20 May and 6 June, Leave led in six. Will Straw, Executive Director of Britain Stronger in Europe, admitted that the focus on immigration was 'snuffing out our opportunity to talk about the economy'.[11] The Remain camp had no credible retort.

The resonance achieved by the core Leave messages, in other words, was crucial in shaping the debate.

Money, migrants and control

As with any popular vote, it is worth paying disproportionate attention to the promises made by the winning side, if only because these are more likely to shape subsequent policy. The Referendum was, of course, a slightly strange case in this regard, as none of those on the Leave side was in a position to deliver directly on the pledges they made. Indeed, most Leave-backing Conservatives were adamant that, in the event that they were victorious, David Cameron should stay on as Prime Minister.

That said, not only were the messages of the Leave camp key to their success in the Referendum itself, but they continued to resonate long after the Referendum had been won. And they drew on themes that had long haunted debates about Britain's EU membership.

Once again, the question of sovereignty, or 'control', as the campaign effectively branded it, was central. The ability of the EU to pass laws binding on the UK, exemplified by the role of the European Court of Justice, had been a persistent source of irritation. Indeed, as we saw in chapter 1, ninety-five Conservative MPs had backed legislation in January 2014 that would have allowed the House of Commons to challenge that authority. Apart from anything else, this debate illustrated a profound misunderstanding of the relationship between rules and markets, but that is a discussion for another day.

Control became a key theme of the campaign. Michael Gove declared that 'the decisions which govern all our lives, the laws we must all obey and the taxes we must all pay should be decided by people we choose and who we can throw out if we want change'.[12] Boris Johnson was, as ever, willing to add some colour to the picture, describing how Brexit would allow the UK to dump lots of 'useless' EU rules, including, he claimed (wrongly), that bananas could only be sold in bunches of two or three, and then only if they were sufficiently straight.

The Leave side also focused on the sums of money the UK sent to the EU. Whatever the truth (or, rather, otherwise) of the £350-million-per-week claim emblazoned on the side of their infamous battle bus, it served its purpose. This was despite the fact that on only one occasion did Vote Leave make the 'error' of explicitly promising the entire £350 million to the NHS.[13] The failure of the Remain side to do anything but argue that the actual sum was smaller ('only' £250 million per week), or to link these payments effectively to the (far larger) economic benefits derived from EU membership, merely served to emphasize that the UK paid the EU an awful lot of money.

Finally, of course, there was immigration, a key issue

in British politics and one that, as we have seen, had been coming to shape attitudes towards the EU itself. UKIP, naturally, could be relied upon to hammer away at this theme, which they duly did.

Immigration also, however, came to be central to the Vote Leave campaign. Conservative Brexiters were only too happy, following the Referendum, to claim that their prospectus had been solidly internationalist, based on an acceptance that immigration brings benefits and even that 'we want more of it'.[14] This is simply not true. As the Referendum approached, Vote Leave increasingly focused on EU immigration. As early as 13 May, John Major was moved to warn the Tory Brexiters of the danger of 'morphing into UKIP'. Despite Fraser Nelson's subsequent claim that Tory Leavers 'did not repeat' David Cameron's pledge to reduce migration to the tens of thousands, they absolutely did. Michael Gove argued precisely that leaving the EU could enable the government to meet its immigration target.[15] Former Europe Minister David Davis was even moved to suggest that immigration could fall to almost zero if Britain left the EU.[16]

The twin issues of money and migration allowed the Leave camp to tap into pre-existing popular concerns. A letter from Gove and Johnson to the Prime Minister (clearly mis-addressed as it ended up splashed on the front page of the *Sunday Times*) pointed out that the government's failure to cut net immigration to the tens of thousands not only was 'corrosive of public trust in politics', but also was undermining the health and education systems.[17]

This in turn points to another crucial miscalculation made by the Remain campaign. They assumed that their talk of the dangers of Brexit in terms of GDP, public finance black holes and the like was generating concern about the economy. In fact, the Leave campaign proved successful in linking economic concerns to the danger of remaining *within* the EU. Attributing the state of public services or falling wages to immigration was an unambiguously economic argument, as were claims about how public services could benefit from a Brexit dividend if payments to the EU budget were stopped.

While the message itself mattered, the debate also hinged on levels of trust in the messengers. In this sense, the campaign reflected the degree to which, as we've shown in chapter 2, trust in politicians, and in 'expert' pronouncements, had declined.

Facts, farce and fiction

Those charged with making the case for remaining within the EU assumed from the start (and in keeping with both received social science wisdom and the apparent lessons of the Scottish independence referendum) that caution would carry the day in the vote to come. By the time the Britain Stronger in Europe organization was launched in October 2015, it had settled on the message that Britain would be 'stronger, safer and better off' in the EU, while leaving represented a 'leap in the dark'.

According to Andrew Cooper, David Cameron's Director of Strategy at Number 10, undecided voters were:

> defined by the fact that they are risk averse. They want facts. They want serious arguments. What [Boris] is

doing . . . is talking to their hearts. . . . They agree with him and they will cheer him for saying it, but that's not enough to get them to leave the European Union.[18]

The official Leave campaign, for its part, also drew on the experience of previous – albeit different – campaigns. The No to AV campaign, headed, as was Vote Leave, by Matthew Elliott, had targeted the cost of a new voting system. Prefiguring the famous red bus, advertisements were taken out in regional newspapers showing a baby with the caption 'She needs a new cardiac facility not an alternative vote system.' Vote Leave adopted similar tactics.

So while Remain focused on facts, even at the cost of running a rather dry and emotionless campaign, their adversaries adopted a more visceral approach. And this was true even at the level of slogans, where 'Stronger, Better off and Safer in Europe' proved no match for 'Take Back Control' or 'Be Leave'.

In keeping with its self-proclaimed status as an anti-establishment insurgency, the Leave campaign was happy to garner publicity by all available means. These ranged from persuading two students to interrupt the Prime Minister's speech at the Confederation of British Industry (CBI) annual conference of November 2015, to the repeated flaunting of the £350 million suppos-edly paid to the EU, to the various stunts carried out by Leave.EU funder Arron Banks, who self-consciously seemed to model his approach on that adopted by Donald Trump in the USA.

Not that Banks was alone in resorting to colourful language. The (perhaps inevitable) references to Hitler duly appeared, as Boris Johnson argued that the EU was pursuing similar goals to those of the German dictator.[19] Meanwhile, Michael Gove rather bizarrely compared experts warning about Brexit to the Nazis who attempted to smear Albert Einstein. The contrast with the Remain campaign could hardly have been more stark. The 'Stronger In' strategy consisted of deploying a barrage of arguments about the economy, delivered by a coterie of national and international experts ranging from the Treasury, to the IMF, to representatives of major corporations, to President Obama.

This tactic, however, quickly ran into problems. In the first place, the message did not resonate with voters, not least because of its negativity. The argument was not that life would improve if Britain remained in the EU, but that Brexit would be costly. The Leave campaign were quick to coin the phrase 'Project Fear'. Indeed, negativity was so persistent that Remain voters themselves expected the economy to worsen even if the UK voted to stay in the EU.[20] Not for nothing did Boris Johnson brand his opponents as the 'Gerald Ratner[s] of modern politics' – accepting, as they appeared to, that the EU was 'crap', while maintaining there was no alternative to it.

Second, in an attempt to achieve some resonance for their arguments, the Remain camp increasingly resorted to exaggeration and hyperbole. On 18 April, the Treasury released a report on the long-term impact of leaving the EU. This examined various scenarios that might succeed EU membership, including a Canada-type trade deal and a WTO-style arrangement, estimating the impact of each on the economy and the public finances.[21] As a piece of economic forecasting, the report was sensible enough, albeit with the caveats that should accompany long-term forecasting of this kind. What was less so was the attempt to place a precise number on the impact per household fifteen years into the future. For the record, the Treasury claimed that each household would be £2,600 worse off than if we'd stayed in the EU in the event of membership of the European Economic Area – the 'Norway' option; £4,300 in the case of a bilateral trade deal with the EU ('Canada'); and £5,200 if relations with the EU were regulated by the World Trade Organization alone. This kind of spurious specificity, from a campaign that had, to this point, argued that uncertainty was the greatest threat that Brexit posed, undermined its credibility.

The Treasury compounded its error just over a month later (23 May), when it published its analysis of the probable short-term impact of a vote to Leave. On the day of publication, the front page of its website declared that a vote to leave the EU would 'tip Britain's economy into a year-long recession', with at least 500,000 jobs lost and GDP around 3.6 per cent lower than it would otherwise have been.[22] This both misrepresented the analysis on which it was based, and was clearly highly partisan in the context of the campaign. Not satisfied with this, on 15 June, in what appeared even at the time as an act of some desperation, the Chancellor appeared alongside his Labour predecessor Alistair Darling to declare that a vote to leave the EU would be followed by an emergency budget in which taxes would rise and spending would be slashed. The damage wrought by these claims, as we shall see, persisted long after the Referendum itself.

Little wonder the Leave camp ramped up its accusations of scaremongering. Increasingly hysterical claims of economic doom had the effect of undermining the credibility of even the serious analyses that lay behind them. Nor was hyperbole confined to the economy. On 9 May, Cameron made a major speech on the security implications of EU membership. In what he actually said, he emphasized the role the EU had played in preserving security on the continent and hinted that Brexit might put this at risk. Significantly more sensational was the previous day's briefing to journalists, which led *The Times* to announce on its front page that 'Brexit will raise risk of world war, PM claims.'

Simultaneously, Cameron's opponents were themselves stretching the limits of the plausible. We've discussed the £350 million issue. So too have we touched on the fact that the Leave campaign was in no position to deliver on the policy pledges it made. Meanwhile, Penny Mordaunt's claim that the UK could not (as opposed to would not) block Turkish membership of the EU was palpably false.

What transpired was that both sides ended up being taken to task. The Head of the UK Statistics Authority complained about the claim that £350 million was sent to the EU weekly. Meanwhile, Andrew Tyrie, Chair of the Commons Treasury Select Committee, urged the Remain campaign to remove from their literature the 'intellectually dishonest' claim that EU membership was worth £3,000 to each household.

Slowly but surely, the idea took root that both sides were lying. It was an assumption that chimed nicely with the prevailing mood about politics described in the previous chapter. And this sense that no one could be trusted was merely intensified by the effectiveness of the Leave camp in playing the man not the ball.

Those academics and think tanks that pointed out the risks of Brexit were routinely branded 'EU-funded sock puppets'. Meanwhile, senior politicians openly attacked key state institutions. In May, Iain Duncan Smith referred to the Treasury as the 'worst thing we have in Britain'. Just over a week before the Referendum itself, on 15 June, he, along with another former Tory leader, Michael Howard, and former Chancellors Lawson and Lamont accused both the Treasury and the Bank of England of 'peddling phony forecasts'.

Perhaps most famously, Michael Gove was heard to declare on national television that the country had 'had enough of experts'. His comments, whilst frequently taken out of context, struck a nerve, not least in a context of declining faith in politics and in the ability of politicians to deliver on their promises.

A neat example of this was provided by a lady in Newcastle. At a public debate immediately prior to the Referendum, one of us was discussing the economic arguments for and against Brexit. He explained that most attempts to model the likely implications had concluded that it would lead to a reduction in GDP. No sooner were the words out of his mouth when the lady in question yelled back 'That's your bloody GDP, not mine.'

It was a telling line. And one that neatly epitomized not only an increasingly cynical attitude towards expertise, but, more specifically, a belief that, whilst pro-Remain politicians might not necessarily be lying, they were describing a reality from another planet (the prosperous South-East). And the data bear out such cynicism – hence talk of economic recovery from the financial crisis was liable to be met with laughter outside of the M25.[23] Equally, while the aggregate economic impact of immigration has been positive, statements to that effect failed to convince people on the wrong side of the economic fence, or those who saw (or thought they saw) increases in migrant numbers directly impacting on their daily lives.

None of which is to say, as Jonathan Portes has repeatedly and patiently explained, that we should not trust the aggregate data.[24] But the fact is that many people did not, or simply found it irrelevant. And this significantly undermined the strategy of the Remain camp, whilst playing into the hands of a Leave campaign that skilfully capitalized on such doubts and anxieties and was focused less on fact than on emotions.

By 25 May, sensing trouble ahead, Ryan Coetzee, Director of Strategy for the Stronger In campaign, was moved to send an email to senior campaign staff stating that

> Voters are very sceptical about our warnings on the economy. They don't trust these reports. They don't trust the numbers. They don't trust the Treasury. And many don't like the messengers.[25]

It was all too indicative of the fate of the Remain campaign, and of the panic that had afflicted it by its latter stages, that, by the time of the ITV debate on 9 June, Amber Rudd, Nicola Sturgeon and Angela Eagle were reduced to launching personal attacks on Boris Johnson.

Beyond party politics?

As the campaigns became increasingly personalized, so, too, did they impact on traditional party loyalties. As we discussed in the preceding chapter, these had been progressively eroded over the previous two decades. The Referendum campaign merely reinforced this trend. For one thing, it crystallized a division in society not represented by the major parties. The Referendum did not divide people along traditional left–right lines, but, rather, centred on values. And, as we've seen, the battle between social liberals and social conservatives cuts across party lines.[26]

Divisions in the Conservative Party over Europe meant that prominent figures were always going to feature in both camps. When it came to the campaign, however, the Prime Minister was reluctant to engage in 'blue-on-blue' attacks on Conservative colleagues. His focus – somewhat hubristically – was on the need to reunite the party once the Referendum had been won. And so a poster featuring Boris Johnson in Nigel Farage's pocket (modelled on the one of Ed Miliband in Alex Salmond's pocket that had proven so effective during the General Election campaign) was ultimately not deployed. As one Downing Street source put it, there was 'a sense that we were bringing knives to a gun battle'.[27] Matthew Elliott subsequently expressed his surprise at this, arguing that linking the two senior Tory defectors to UKIP as 'crazy, right-wing nutters' would have proved 'terminal' for the Vote Leave campaign he ran.[28]

In stark contrast, the Leave side exploited the 'blue-on-blue' dynamic assiduously. They took every opportunity to attack the government and its record, which both earned them extensive media coverage and contributed to the gradual erosion of trust in Cameron and Osborne. Not incidentally, the fascination of the media with Conservative in-fighting also had the effect of making supporters of other parties lose interest in the Referendum campaign.

The policy pledges announced by Vote Leave as purdah kicked in were a deliberate ploy intended to play on the fact that the media's main concern was with the identity of the next Prime Minister. What, after all, could be juicier than the sight of leading politicians setting out an alternative manifesto from within the same government as the Prime Minister?[29]

At the same time, the Leave camp skilfully crafted a populist appeal designed to tap into the kind of suspicions about politics and politicians described in the previous chapter. Boris Johnson wrote – graphically – about the 'vast clerisy of lobbyists and corporate affairs gurus – all the thousands of Davos men and women who have their jaws firmly clamped around the euro-teat'.[30] He went on to point out not only that the rich are not exposed to the pressures caused by large-scale immigration, but that they use EU regulation to maintain their oligarchic position.[31]

Events conspired to reinforce these messages. In March 2016, Work and Pensions Minister Iain Duncan Smith resigned in the wake of the budget, in protest (he said) at the tax cuts delivered to higher earners. Tellingly, he accused the Chancellor, George Osborne, of undermining the claim that 'We are all in this together.' Less than a month later, in early April, both the revelations about the business – and particularly tax – affairs of the Prime Minister's father contained in the Panama Papers, and Cameron's own inept handling of the media storm around it, further undermined the PM's credibility.

Tensions within the Conservative Party reached a peak as George Osborne declared on 15 June that, in the event of a Brexit vote, he would deliver an emergency budget to plug an expected £30 billion black hole in the public finances. In response, fifty-seven Tory MPs, including former Cabinet ministers, issued a statement pledging to vote the budget down and declaring it absurd to make a political promise to punish voters – and to break Conservative manifesto promises into the bargain.

If what the Tories stood for was not clear, this was true in spades for the Labour Party. Remain needed to attract Labour voters inherently suspicious of a Prime Minister whose policies had, in many cases, made them worse off. Yet the new party leadership under Jeremy Corbyn was, to put it mildly, far from convinced of the benefits of EU membership.

Corbyn himself was soon accused of sabotaging the Remain campaign. He refused to focus on – or even plan for – the Referendum until after the local elections in May. His team cut pro-EU lines from his speeches (the phrase 'that's why I'm campaigning to remain in the EU' was reportedly a frequent victim of such editing), and he avoided events organized by the Labour In group. Corbyn's office even arranged a visit to Turkey to talk about the value of open borders (just imagine, in the context of a campaign dominated by immigration), though opposition from within the party led to its cancellation.[32]

Private polling apparently clearly showed that a public appearance by Corbyn and Cameron together would be the 'number one play' to reach Labour voters.[33] However, despite senior staff from the Remain campaign – including Gordon Brown – begging him to attend a rally with the Prime Minister, the Labour leader flatly refused.

Gordon Brown also proposed that Corbyn should make a public appearance with former Labour leaders. The latter again refused, this time because of his reluctance to share a platform with Tony Blair – even when the latter's participation was downgraded merely to a statement read by someone else.

Disagreement also extended to substantive issues. Corbyn, Brown and Hilary Benn expounded on the benefits of migration without controls, whilst Yvette Cooper and Tom Watson argued in favour of a revision of EU rules on free movement. As the campaign unfolded, Labour MPs encountered strong public discontent about immigration but were unable to point to a single, clear party position on the issue. One Stronger In staffer was quoted as saying that they 'understand that Labour needs to sort out its immigration policy. But the time to do it is not a week before polling day on live fucking television.'[34]

Meanwhile, Corbyn frequently attacked what was nominally his own side. He argued that Treasury forecasts about the consequences of a vote to Leave were 'histrionic'. Following a speech at the start of June (in which he accused both sides of 'myth making'), the top Google search for him was 'Does he want in or out?' According to internal polling just weeks before the vote, one in five Labour voters did not know the party's position on the Referendum.

While the parties squabbled amongst themselves, the Referendum also generated unexpected alliances. Labour MP Gisela Stuart was a prominent figure chairing the Vote Leave campaign. Meanwhile, her colleague Kate Hoey was happy to share platforms with UKIP leader Nigel Farage.

Perhaps more importantly, however, the Remain campaign brought together what one insider referred to as the 'pluralist, liberal, centrist force in British politics'. *Guardian* journalist Rafael Behr labelled these people, who hailed from the Conservatives, Labour and the Liberal Democrats, the ruling class of 'Remainia'. As he points out, prior to the rise of UKIP and Jeremy Corbyn, these individuals had conducted political debate in terms of 'shades of difference within a broad consensus'.[35]

This tallies with our analysis in the preceding chapter. And, crucially, the Referendum gave those people who felt overlooked by this centrist elite the perfect opportunity to register their dissatisfaction in a way that the 'first past the post' voting system used for General Elections simply did not. The Stronger In campaign represented an easy target for opponents willing to tap into popular concerns about the direction of politics and the state of the economy. The steady drift towards disillusionment and distrust finally came back to haunt the political establishment.

A change is gonna come

Many of the key themes we identified in chapters 1 and 2 came to the fore during the Referendum campaign. The Leave camp proved successful at manipulating a host of popular concerns about public spending, the economy and, above all, immigration. Just as importantly, they sensed and promoted the anti-establishment feelings of a population increasingly frustrated with its political elite.

The campaign also witnessed an unprecedented

level of hostility towards key institutions, such as the Treasury, and expert bodies such as the IMF and World Bank. The role of experts and of expertise was called into question, raising the prospect of a more visceral politics in place of the evidence-, or at least expertise-, based approach that had become the norm under New Labour.

Finally, the campaign prefigured what is now turning into a profound recalibration of British politics. The blurring of party lines, as well as the coalescence and defeat of the liberal 'Remainia' elite that had governed the country since the late 1990s, both pointed to the unsustainability of that model, an impression heightened by the ambivalent attitude adopted by the Labour Party leadership.

But before all that could play out, the British had to go to the polls.

4

Voting to Leave

We have, up to this point, sketched the context in which the Referendum took place: the persistent unease about EU membership, the weak sense of identification with Europe that had characterized the UK since it joined, declining commitment to mainstream political parties, low levels of trust in politicians and a campaign that played deliberately upon these themes. In this chapter, we focus more specifically on why people voted the way they did on the day and what this implied for Britain's politics going forward.

Inevitably, public attitudes towards the European Union were enormously important, and shaped voters' responses to the frenetic Referendum campaign. Widespread euroscepticism existed across society, as did concerns about immigration which, as we have seen, was a key issue during the campaign.

But this is not enough to explain the outcome. The erosion of faith in politics described in chapter 2 also played its part. Leave supporters ignored virtually the whole British – and indeed international – establishment to vote in favour of leaving the European Union.

Decreasing attachment to parties, declining trust in politicians, and increasing scepticism about the claims made by self-professed experts all contributed to ensuring that people simply were not as open to persuasion as they had been in 1975. Roy Jenkins once explained the outcome of that Referendum on EC membership by arguing that the British electorate 'took the advice of people they were used to following'.[1] By 2016, they were far less inclined to do so.

Above all, the Referendum revealed a country divided. Divided over values, divided by class, by generation, education and geography. And these divisions will continue to shape our politics for the foreseeable future.

Euroscepticism and values

Rather than coolly weighing the prospective costs and benefits of leaving, via a careful examination of the competing claims made by the campaigns, most voters appear to have made up their minds beforehand. Those who, for whatever reason, had not liked the European Union continued to dislike it, and those who had, continued to do so. Evidence concerning what people thought Brexit might mean in a number of different areas, ranging from unemployment to international trade to immigration and terrorism, is revealing in this respect. Those who thought Brexit would have a positive impact in one area thought it would in other areas too, while those who thought it would have a negative impact in one area thought it would do so in all others. This is obvious from table 4.1.

There is little in the way of common ground here –

Table 4.1 What would Brexit mean? (Percentage of people who felt each outcome was 'likely or very likely')

	Remain voters		Leave voters	
	Pre-campaign	During campaign	Pre-campaign	During campaign
'Higher unemployment'	55	58	9	7
'Less international trade'	64	65	7	6
'Higher immigration'	13	12	7	6
'Higher risk of terrorism'	34	37	8	7
'Less British influence'	67	71	8	7
'Poorer working conditions'	53	58	5	4
'Weaker economy'	68	76	4	5
'Worse personal financial situation'	40	45	4	4
'Big businesses will leave Britain'	71	74	8	8

Source: British Election Study panel surveys (pre-campaign and campaign waves).

almost nothing that is not dismissed by one side yet feared by the other – with the exception of immigration, of which more below. The crucial point is that, in the minds of the public, EU membership was either a good thing or a bad thing. Nuanced arguments about its impact in specific areas of British life had little or no influence on these opinions.

An explanation for this lack of impact can be found in the fact that these generalized expectations were rooted in attitudes towards the EU that had been formed years earlier. Before the official campaign had even kicked off, many people had made up their minds. Remarkably, some 80 per cent of Referendum votes could be predicted by referring to responses to a single question about the EU posed in 2010.[2] In the often volatile world of individual political attitudes, this was a remarkable level of stability.

These rock-solid attitudes to the EU also have a basis in values. As we mentioned in chapter 2, when talking about values we're not referring to the traditional bread-and-butter issues of politics – redistribution, the NHS, welfare payments and so on. Rather, we mean the difference between those with socially conservative beliefs and those with more socially liberal views on questions of order, authority, morality and freedom. In chapter 2, we described how the main parties had coalesced around a broadly liberal position that was not closely representative of the beliefs of many people. The Referendum brought this situation to a head. These values could now be expressed through the ballot box.

And if we look at the connection between these values and the Referendum vote the picture – literally – is clear. Figure 4.1 shows the powerful link between social

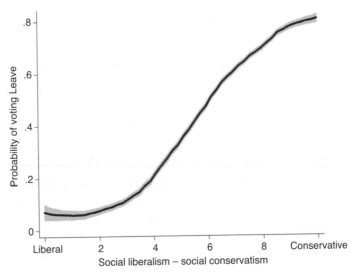

Figure 4.1 Values and the Referendum

Source: BES.

values and votes in the Referendum. No fewer than 80 per cent of the most socially conservative voters opted to Leave, compared to fewer than 10 per cent of the most socially liberal. And these findings tally with those produced by a NatCen study, which found that 66 per cent of those with socially conservative views voted to Leave, compared with only 18 per cent of social liberals.[3]

In chapter 2, we referred to attitudes towards the death penalty to flag up the differences between public opinion and the positions of the main parties when it came to values. In the Referendum itself, around three-quarters of those who back capital punishment voted to Leave, compared to only about 20 per cent of those who oppose it.

The thing about values is that they don't change much. They provide what can best be thought of as a bedrock to political beliefs which shapes these beliefs over the long term. And because values were so central to the Referendum, it should come as little surprise that the attitudes of voters were remarkably stable over time.

Thus, polls suggest that the balance of support for Leave and Remain changed comparatively little during the two years prior to the Referendum. Both hovered at around 40 per cent until the summer of 2015. After this, opinion began to crystallize, with a declining proportion of people answering 'don't know' when asked how they intended to vote.[4] Even so, there is little in the way of evidence that the campaigns played a significant role in *changing* minds. Analysis of no less than 121 Internet and phone polls carried out between 11 January and 22 June 2016 found that Leave may well have had the lead throughout the entire campaign.[5]

This gels with what we've said about the Referendum campaign itself. Increasingly, it appeared that both campaigns were engaged in peddling exaggeration and hyperbole. Little wonder that many voters tended to fall back upon their long-held views.

The one issue where the public seemed liable to be persuaded was owned by Leave. Perhaps the only undisputed fact in the campaign was that controlling immigration would be far more difficult from within the EU. Think back to table 4.1. The one thing Leavers and Remainers could agree on was that immigration would not go up in the event of Brexit. Even Remainers accepted that Brexit would reduce immigration. Staying in the EU would mean that Britain could not prevent EU citizens from coming to Britain. Indeed, David Cameron's failure to bring about meaningful change via his much-vaunted renegotiation merely underlined this fact.

Predictably enough, then, immigration and sovereignty were the most frequently cited issues among those who voted Leave. And among people with a negative view of immigration, no fewer than 80 per cent voted to leave the EU.[6] In contrast, Remain voters cared about the economic implications of leaving. The remarkable degree to which the preoccupations of the two sides differed was dramatically illustrated by the 'word clouds' first shown on ITV on the night of the Referendum itself (see figure 4.2). These word clouds reflect the number of times people mentioned different sorts of issues when they were asked to say *in their own words* what was motivating their vote.[7]

So there we have it in their own words: Leave voters were concerned about immigration along with – to a lesser extent – control, sovereignty and country. Remainers, for their part, were overwhelmingly concerned about the economic consequences of Brexit along with its impact on employment and social rights.

Immigration mattered not only at the level of personal beliefs but also when it came to (some measures of) external reality. Sophisticated area-level analyses have found that those areas that had experienced a recent influx of migrants from the countries that joined the EU in 2004 and 2007 were more likely to vote Leave. Interestingly, those where similar increases had occurred from other countries were not.[8]

The same studies also illustrate that poverty and inequality were important. Former manufacturing areas, and those where levels of pay were relatively low and levels of unemployment relatively high, were all more likely to favour Leave. Leave votes were high in

Leave voters:

Remain voters:

Figure 4.2 'What matters most to you when deciding how to vote?'

Source: BES.

areas with poor public service provision – themselves often the result of the cuts associated with austerity. And the proportion of the population with few or no qualifications was a particularly strong predictor of the Vote Leave share.[9]

Most intriguingly of all, however, immigration and the economy were inter-connected. Where Eastern European migrants had settled in areas with both more manufacturing workers and less well-educated populations, there were higher numbers of Leave votes.

In contrast, areas with higher levels of income where such migrants had settled saw an increased vote for Remain.[10] Presumably, in the former, migrants would be seen as competing for jobs and services, whereas in the latter, they provide (cheap) labour and services for those who can afford them.

So what of the campaign?

As we've said, support for Leave and Remain changed relatively little during the two years prior to the Referendum. There was no shift towards the Leave camp during the campaign itself. If anything, the Remain campaign picked up more votes at the tail end (51 per cent, as opposed to only 45 per cent for Leave) from amongst the few remaining 'Don't knows' – spurred perhaps by the fall-out from the murder of MP Jo Cox.[11]

This, however, should not be taken to imply that the campaigns did not matter (or that you've wasted your time by reading the previous chapter). It is something of a truism in the study of referendums that voters tend to stick with the status quo when confronted with a choice between that and the unknown. As we've seen, this was certainly the assumption made by the Remain campaign. And Scotland's referendum a couple of years earlier appeared to provide evidence that it was the case. The term 'status quo bias' has been coined by social scientists for this phenomenon, which is taken to reflect a general tendency to be risk averse amongst populations.

Certainly, the 'experts' expected such a bias would ultimately produce a victory for Remain. Eminent pollster Peter Kellner was of the opinion that polls generally come out in favour of the 'no change' option, opining that history 'favours remain'.[12] On the day of the vote itself, no less a figure than the Head of the UK Statistics Authority informally predicted a 55% plus vote in favour of remaining in the EU. This consensus included one of us, who confidently informed the CBI that 'risk-averse voters would not vote for the unknown', and blithely put £1,100 of his own money (no laughing matter on an academic salary) where his mouth was.

How wrong we were. Indeed, even more so than may at first meet the eye. Insofar as people tend to be risk averse, those who are generally most so are the elderly, the poorly educated, and the not-very-well-off. Yet these were the very groups that came out most strongly in favour of leaving the EU.

So how did this happen? One reason is that the Brexiters successfully undermined the notion of the status quo. Leave campaigners emphasized that remaining within the European Union was not the stable or predictable option.

In the first place, they pointed out that migration was rising (the ONS figures that appeared at the end of May were a Godsend in this regard). They were also happy – albeit indirectly – to link the issue of migration from the EU to the danger of terrorism. They were helped in this by the images of the migration crisis on our TV screens in the months running up to the campaign. Meanwhile, Michael Gove, as we have seen, raised the spectre of an imminent EU enlargement leading to even greater numbers of EU citizens coming to the UK.[13]

Leave campaigners also argued that the EU itself was an organization in perpetual movement towards closer integration. As Daniel Haman put it:

All the integrationist measures that have been put in the fridge pending our referendum would come tumbling out. First, the directives that have already been drawn up. . . . Then, soon afterwards, we'll get to the bigger things: the budget hike, the harmonization of taxation and social security provision, the gradual creation of an EU military capacity. There'll be no point protesting: we'll have voted to stay in knowing that they were on the agenda.[14]

Thus, the notion that remaining within the EU represented a stable status quo was subtly yet systematically undermined. The message was simple: those who were risk averse would be better off voting to Leave. The alternative was to vote for an increase in immigration and a swift and relentless journey to an EU superstate. In all this, of course, the Leave camp was aided by the failure of its opponents to mention the Prime Minister's renegotiation and the concessions he'd managed to extract, particularly when it came to the EU's commitment to 'ever closer union'.

The success of the Leave campaign can arguably also be seen in the impressive levels of turnout achieved among its supporters. Some 3 million more people – almost 10% of the electorate – turned out to vote on 23 June 2016 than did in the General Election in May 2015. Noticeably, this increase was most marked amongst social groups with a preference for leaving the EU.

Turnout was still relatively low in those areas with large numbers of people with no educational qualifications (68.9%). Yet these areas actually witnessed a larger increase in turnout (8.4 percentage points) than did those containing large numbers of middle-class graduates (6.6 percentage points).[15] Indeed, the estimated 'participation gap' between highly educated profession-als (typically Remain) and people in manual jobs with lower levels of education (typically Leave) referred to in chapter 2 was reduced from 39% in 2015 to only 20%.[16] Intriguingly, a recent NatCen report has also found that people who leant towards Remain in the lead up to the Referendum were significantly more likely to abstain on the day (19%) than were Leave supporters (11%).[17]

And the parties?

The political parties were the dogs that didn't bark in the Referendum. Although the leaders of the main par-ties strongly – or weakly, in the case of Jeremy Corbyn – advocated Remain, their voters proved less than wholly convinced. The BES shows that a striking 61% of Conservative supporters voted Leave (36% voted Remain). For Labour, the figures were roughly reversed – 34% Leave and 61% Remain. Almost half (48%) of all Leave voters were Conservatives, while only 29% were Labour supporters. Even the Liberal Democrats, tradi-tionally the most pro-EU of the major national parties, saw almost a quarter (24%) of their supporters opting for Leave. Brexit, in other words, divided the parties to an unusual degree. Only UKIP – unsurprisingly – was spared: 94% of its supporters backed the party line.

There are two main reasons why the parties did not mobilize their followers to the degree we might have expected. First, the social values that played such a cru-cial role in generating the outcome of the Referendum did not correspond to the usual left–right divisions. Thus,

Leave voters were pretty equally divided between those on the right and left of the traditional political spectrum (53% versus 50%, respectively).[18] These values therefore cut across traditional party lines, especially when it came to the two larger parties.

Second, as we have already seen, there had been a decline in party identification, increasing voter volatility, and a growing distance between parties and the public. Faith in politicians had reached worryingly low levels in the years leading up to the Referendum. These attitudes showed no signs of changing as the vote approached. At the end of March, people were asked 'Who do you trust on issues relating to the referendum on EU membership?' The results were unambiguous. While academics (obviously) scored highly (trusted by 69% of Remain supporters and 50% of Leave voters), both camps placed most faith in friends and family. Only 12% of Remainers and 9% of Leavers trusted 'politicians generally'.[19]

By April, MORI found that only 9% of those asked thought that politicians would honour the promises made in the campaign, while 10% thought these promises were realistic. A mere 23% believed politicians were explaining their policies clearly enough to allow voters to make up their minds. The political establishment was simply not trusted by those it was trying to convince.

This mattered enormously. The signal from most politicians, across all parties bar one, backed by a coterie of national and international experts from venerable institutions ranging from the IMF to the Bank of England, was that Britain would be better advised to remain within the EU. But their influence and standing was not what it once was. Indeed, given the endemic scepticism about the establishment, its condemnation of Brexit may even have stiffened some people's resolve to vote for it. So the government, with enormous resources at its disposal, failed to sway the vote. And both major parties failed to bring enough of their voters over with them. This alone underlines the decreasing influence of the political establishment over those it governs. When push came to shove, the parties could not deliver.

The social fabric of Brexit

As ever in British politics, social class had a role to play in this story, albeit not necessarily in quite the way some have claimed. Much has been written about how Brexit was the result of a revolt by 'the left behind'. There is some truth to this, but it is an over-simplification.

Some 63% of the working class voted to Leave, compared with only 44% of the middle class. Even when the effects of age, region, race, religion, gender and housing are taken into account, there was still a 10 percentage point gap between the working class and the professional middle class.[20] Areas characterized as 'white British working class' were those most likely to have voted to leave the EU.[21]

The gulf between the working class, and particularly the less highly educated, and other social groups when it comes to immigration is even greater than that over the traditional core issues of politics – inequality and redistribution.[22] The working class are often described as (and, in many cases, are) the 'losers from globalization', or the 'left behind'. Compared to the university-educated, they tend to be more rooted in their local and national communities and face stiffer labour market competition from migrants.[23]

The impact of education was still more striking, however. No fewer than 72% of those with no educational qualifications voted to Leave, compared with only 35% of people with a university degree. There was a remarkable 30 percentage point gap between those with low versus those with high levels of education even when all other factors were taken into account.[24]

Yet it was not merely the less-highly educated and the working class who brought Brexit about. Given the relatively reduced size of the modern-day working class, substantial numbers of the middle classes had to vote Leave to ensure a result in favour of Brexit. The BES shows that the proportion of Leave voters doing routine and semi-routine jobs – the core of the working class – was only 21%. In contrast, the proportion of Leave voters from lower professional jobs alone was 27%, intermediate administrative posts and the like made up 23%, employers and the self-employed 11%. It was the often highly educated middle classes that provided the major source – some 59% in total – of the Brexit vote.

Age also mattered. Over 40% of the Leave vote was aged over 55. The elderly are unlikely to be found in urban areas and it's not hard to understand why so many market towns and seaside resorts were solidly anti-EU. Here, we are not just talking about the 'left behind', but about those feeling 'left out' – people whose views are out of step with dominant liberal political values.

In contrast, young people were heavily pro-Remain, but were also less likely to turn out and vote.[25] It would be wrong to infer that lazy youngsters were in some way responsible for the outcome, however. In the UK, 18- to 24-year-olds make up only around 11% of the voting population.[26] To overturn the result, it has been calculated that some 120% of them would have had to have voted (rather than the 64% who actually did). Even to the less quantitatively minded of the two of us, this seems a tall order. Even if we stretch the definition of 'young' to those under 45 (which is a nice idea), the story is not wholly dissimilar. Turnout among this population would have had to have been an unprecedented 97%, rather than the 65% it actually was, to have changed the result.[27]

In sum, the vote to Leave was a result of a broad-based social coalition. NatCen's incisive recent analysis concluded that this coalition incorporated at least three main groups: affluent eurosceptics, the older working class, and a smaller group of economically disadvantaged, anti-immigration voters.[28]

One further conclusion that we might draw from looking at the who and why of voting for Brexit concerns the failure of the much-vaunted educational expansion of recent years to have changed our country to the extent that many have assumed. People with university degrees certainly displayed by far the strongest level of support for Remain. Indeed, they provided over half (51%) of Remain's votes. But, even now, only around one quarter of the population have a university degree. Even among the young, most people do not have degrees, and this applies even more among the old. And the electorate is increasingly elderly – through longer life expectancy and the tendency in recent decades to have fewer children. The impact of the upsurge in higher education enrolment was simply not sufficient to swing it for Remain.

The seeds of change

To a significant extent, these social divisions account for the geographical distribution of the Brexit vote. And contained in this were clear signals regarding the pattern of electoral politics to come. The Leave versus Remain divide cut across Labour and Conservative constituencies in various ways.

In Lincolnshire, East Anglia and Kent, EU immigrants had settled in relatively dense clusters, providing the backbone of crop-picking and other agricultural work. These traditionally Conservative areas had already seen UKIP garner significant support in 2015, and they formed the rural heartland of the Brexit vote in 2016. So, for example, Wisbech, centre of an extensive arable farming area, saw 71.4% vote to Leave, on a 73.7% turnout. In affluent agricultural Kent, 59% voted to Leave. A raft of Conservative coastal towns with older populations had also seen substantial levels of UKIP voting in 2015, and likewise witnessed Leave victories: Scarborough (62%), Eastbourne (57.3%) and Bournemouth (54.9%).

Alongside these rural and coastal constituencies, smaller cities and Northern towns – traditional Labour heartlands, in other words – also disproportionately voted to Leave. Stoke-on-Trent, dubbed 'Brexit central' during its February 2017 by-election, had a Leave vote of 69.4% on a 65.7% turnout – which was to prove a matter of no little consequence in the General Election to come. On a similar turnout, Sunderland saw 61.3% vote to Leave, while 69.3% in Hartlepool backed Brexit. For Labour, this was a source of great concern, especially given the parlous state of support for the party following Jeremy Corbyn's re-election. And, of course, UKIP had obtained reasonable levels of support in these places in 2015. It was not hard to discern the electoral logic behind Theresa May's approach to Brexit after her coronation in July 2016. It placed both Midlands and Northern working-class Labour Leave-voting seats firmly in play and held out the prospect of killing off UKIP.

London, in contrast, was overwhelmingly pro-Remain, whether in impoverished multi-ethnic Hackney (78.5%) or affluent Kensington & Chelsea (68.7%). But with a 59.9% vote for Remain, the London region as a whole was a marked outlier in Southern England. The affluent South-East had a Leave majority that was identical to that in the country as a whole (51.8%). Other large cities, typically Labour strongholds, had voted to Remain. Manchester (60.4%) voted to stay. So too did Leeds (50.3%). As we were to see in the General Election almost a year later, these regional variations presaged a shift in British political geography.

The electorate's revenge

The Referendum was not a General Election. And it showed what can happen when every vote counts, when choices are clear-cut and relevant, and when parties are unable to blur the differences between these choices. It marked a rejection of the arguments put forward by the majority of the British political establishment.

Many, if not most, people had already made their minds up about how they felt about the EU years before the Referendum. Their votes were influenced by prior convictions rather than an impartial assessment of the arguments put forward by the two campaigns. What the Leave campaign managed to do was undermine the notion that continued membership of the EU would represent stability, to capitalize on prevailing distrust of the political establishment, and to mobilize its supporters on the day. The Leave campaign's other key message was that the Referendum represented an opportunity for ordinary citizens to 'take back control' from remote elites in both Westminster and Brussels. For many voters, the Referendum represented an opportunity to vote against not merely the government of the day, but against the political class as a whole.[29]

The outcome of the campaign was not merely a bloody nose for the main parties, but a further decline in their standing. MORI's 'veracity index' saw the percentage of people who would 'trust politicians to tell the truth' fall from 21 per cent in 2015 to 15 per cent following the Referendum, and a fall in the number of people who trusted government ministers (down to 20 from 22 per cent). Trust in politicians was down to levels last seen during the expenses scandal in 2009.

Social divisions had been exposed, but these divisions were not created by the Referendum, or by Brexit. Britain is not now more divided than hitherto. The Referendum simply gave voice to these longstanding divisions. For the first time since the political transformations of the 1990s, when the main political parties began to converge on the liberal centre ground, it allowed traditionalists, eurosceptics and nationalists, amongst others, to express their preferences effectively through the simple act of voting. When the chance was presented, they were able to 'bite back' and, for the first time in many years, decide the outcome of an important political event. Roy Jenkins must be turning in his grave.

5

The Shaping of Things
to Come

Brexit, as we've seen, was a long time in the making. So much so that the furious campaign that dominated our lives in the first half of 2016 changed surprisingly few minds. The outcome, nonetheless, represented a seismic shock to the British political system. Within a day, the Prime Minister had resigned. Within a week, Nigel Farage had done the same, and Jeremy Corbyn was facing a leadership challenge. Within a month, we had a new Prime Minister. Within a year, a General Election hinted at the redrawing of the political map of Britain.

Two examples serve to illustrate this lattermost point. Kensington & Chelsea – perhaps the most affluent constituency in the country – fell to the Labour Party for the first time ever. Stoke-on-Trent South, a poor area in a struggling former industrial city, went from Labour to the Conservatives – again, for the first time ever.

Brexit has been, and will continue to be, central to these political convulsions. The Referendum, as we have seen, challenged traditional political affiliations. The values divide, which we have discussed in some detail, cut across party lines. Moreover, real political conflict returned to centre stage. Jeremy Corbyn injected ideology back into the Labour Party. Meanwhile, new Prime Minister Theresa May outlined a populist agenda combining a pledge to take the UK out of the EU while clamping down on immigration, with promises to improve the lives of those 'just about managing'.

This chapter differs from those that have preceded it in that some – though far from all – of the ground we cover is necessarily speculative in nature. But it is important to try to address some of the key questions that will shape our country and its politics for some time to come: how will the Remain–Leave divide revealed by the Referendum shape party politics? Are we witnessing the return of ideological competition – profound disagreements over the way our society and economy should be organized? Is two-party politics back to stay? Have we seen a decisive, and sustainable, increase in political participation?

The answers to these questions hinge in large part on what Brexit might mean in practice for the UK. The Referendum was a catalyst for change. The Brexit process will determine precisely what form this change will take.

The Aftermath

The Referendum triggered a period of profound instability in British politics. Immediately after the vote, the Conservative Party found itself roiled by a leadership election in which the various candidates contrived to be pushed out or to drop out, leaving Theresa May the last woman standing. Labour's agonies were more drawn out. Amidst accusations that Jeremy Corbyn had not done enough to campaign against Brexit, a leadership battle was triggered. Following lacklustre challenges by first Angela Eagle then Owen Smith, Corbyn was re-elected with an increased mandate (61.85 per cent of the vote) on 24 September.

UKIP, for its part, staged a pantomime all of its own, as Diane James stepped down as Farage's successor after only eighteen days – prompting a brief return from the latter. There was more to come. New front-runner Steven Woolf was literally knocked out of the race in October by Mike Hookem (*sic*) after an 'altercation' in the European Parliament. Woolf was moved to leave the party, labelling it as 'rotten', 'ungovernable' and in the grip of a 'death spiral'. Finally, in November, Paul Nuttall beat Suzanne Evans to the 'prize'.

While the parties dealt with succession, the British state was being reconfigured for Brexit. Only three days after coming to power, on 14 July, Theresa May instigated the single biggest change to the machinery of Whitehall in living memory, creating a Department for Exiting the European Union and a Department for International Trade and appointing David Davis and Liam Fox, respectively, to head them.

It was a long, febrile summer. Political theatre aside, we witnessed a spike in hate crime directed against immigrants and ethnic minorities, marches and protests and the birth of new campaign groups for and against 'hard' and 'soft' Brexit ('Open Britain', 'Get Britain Out'). Meanwhile, the constitution was tested by a Brazilian-born 37-year-old hairdresser, Deir Dos Santos, and Gina Miller, a 51-year-old investment manager and philanthropist, who lodged a legal complaint against the government's plan to trigger Article 50 of the Lisbon Treaty without a parliamentary vote.

And, amidst all the political in-fighting, the questions of what Brexit actually meant, and of how it would be put into effect, were left deliciously vague. Over those summer months, a host of adjectival alternatives did the rounds – soft Brexit, hard Brexit, managed Brexit, chaotic Brexit, red-white-and-blue Brexit, and (of course) dog's Brexit.

Partly, the lack of clarity stemmed from the complete failure of the previous government to prepare for the contingency of a Brexit vote. Cabinet Secretary Jeremy Heywood assured the Public Administration and Constitutional Affairs Committee of the House of Commons (PACAC) that planning had taken place – in the form of an away-day held without the Prime Minister's knowledge.[1] However, it soon became clear that this was far from sufficient. The Foreign Affairs Committee dubbed the lack of preparation as 'at best naïve and at worst negligent'.[2]

Above and beyond such trivial oversights, confusion was inherent in the Referendum process itself. The binary choice with which voters were presented contained at least four discrete outcomes. First, and most obviously, remaining within the EU. While many Leavers, as we have seen, pointed out that this hardly represented a stable status quo, this was the clearest of all the choices.

Leaving, on the other hand, bundled up a number of options. One possibility was to end EU membership while remaining within the single market. This so-called 'Norway model' promised the least disruption to trade relations with the EU following Brexit. However – and importantly, given the nature of the campaign that led to the vote to Leave – it would have implied being subject to EU law, accepting freedom of movement and continuing to pay into the EU budget.

The second Leave option involved leaving the single market and customs union and signing a bilateral trade deal with the European Union. This 'Canada option' would require Britain and its EU partners to be able to sign a trade deal which would allow for the continuation of as much bilateral commerce as possible without single market and customs union membership.

Finally, option 3 would be simply to rely on World Trade Organization rules to govern bilateral trade with the EU. This 'hard Brexit' scenario, as it has come to be known, would imply a far greater economic impact, to which we will return. Importantly, like the 'Canada option', it would also not only imply an end to (most) payments to the EU budget, but take the UK outside the ambit of EU law, and allow the government to control immigration.

And so the battle over Brexit began. Furious arguments raged concerning its optimal form. These were every bit as intense, if not as all-consuming, as those during the Referendum campaign itself. And rumours were rife. James Landale, the BBC diplomatic correspondent, revealed that pro-Remain MPs were considering using their Commons majority to keep the UK in the single market.[3] There was talk of a need for a second referendum to approve whatever deal was eventually done.

All this was suddenly and decisively brought to a halt in Birmingham in October. Theresa May had already made it clear during the Tory leadership contest that she intended to push ahead with the process of leaving the European Union: 'Brexit', as she famously – and repeatedly – pointed out, 'means Brexit'. Now, with Labour fresh from its leadership battle and struggling to find its voice, she left little room for doubt what she took that to mean. Without mentioning either the single market or the customs union explicitly, her categorical statements that the UK would control immigration, make its own laws, and strike trade deals with third countries – alongside the overt rejection of a 'Norway' or 'Switzerland' model – made it clear that, for her, Brexit meant hard Brexit.

This was not quite the end of the matter. Rumours continued to swirl that the Conservative 'awkward squad' led by Anna Soubry, Nicky Morgan and Ken Clarke were poised to make life difficult for the Prime Minister, and that opposition to May's stance might even extend to her Chancellor, Philip Hammond. By December, manifestations of the Tory rift peaked (or troughed) with 'Trousergate', as Nicky Morgan's criticism of the PM's sartorial choices spawned an undignified slanging match between Leavers and Remainers across the front pages.

In November, the High Court had ruled that parliament was entitled to a vote before the government could trigger Article 50. As the government appealed to the Supreme Court, the governments of Scotland, Wales and Northern Ireland joined Miller and Dos Santos in the case. In a now infamous headline, the *Daily Mail* captured the increasingly ugly public mood, branding High Court Judges 'enemies of the people', while Miller and other 'remoaners' came in for widespread and often personal attack.

Yet what, at one stage, looked like a multifaceted

insurrection ultimately proved ineffective and short-lived. Following a meeting in Downing Street in December, Conservative opposition to Theresa May's Brexit plan appeared to evaporate. Anna Soubry tweeted positively about the Prime Minister's much-heralded Lancaster House speech in January, although this merely reaffirmed Number 10's hard-Brexit approach.

The government's eventual defeat in the Supreme Court on 24 January was ultimately a pyrrhic victory for opponents of Brexit. The subsequent introduction, debate and passing of the Article 50 Bill was anticlimactic in the extreme. Only 47 of 299 Labour MPs defied a three-line whip and voted against the Bill, which passed both houses of parliament unamended, receiving royal assent on 16 March. On 20 March, Theresa May wrote to the President of the European Council to announce her intention to trigger Article 50 and take Britain out of the EU.

Fear no more?

Throughout this period, arguments from the Referendum campaign continued to weigh on the debate. Most significantly, the Treasury's gloom-ridden short-term forecast of the impact of Brexit became the Brexiters' best friend. Dire predictions of job losses and indeed recession proved simply to be false. Even when the pound fell precipitately immediately following the Referendum, it was easy for proponents of Brexit to point out that things were nowhere near as bad as predicted.

Responding to a March 2017 Demos report that raised the prospect of Wales suffering significant economic repercussions as a result of Brexit, a spokesman for Welsh Conservative leader Andrew R. T. Davies remarked acidly that 'According to project fear we should be holed up in a post-apocalyptic wasteland in threadbare clothes eating tinned food by now.' On 2 February 2017, the Bank of England upgraded its economic growth forecast for the second time in six months. All too easy, then, to argue that 'project fear' had got it all wrong.

There was also evidence that public opinion was shifting. A YouGov poll carried out in the first week of May 2017 revealed that, in addition to the two tribes that emerged from the Referendum, a third could be added. While 45 per cent of respondents had backed Brexit and expected the government to take Britain out of the EU, and 22 per cent voted to Remain and believed the government should ignore the Referendum result, or seek to overturn it, a third group of 23 per cent – branded ReLeavers – had backed Remain but now believed the government had a duty to act on the basis of the Referendum result.[4] By the time the government moved to trigger Article 50, 69 per cent of the public favoured this step.[5]

A *new politics*

We remarked in chapter 2 on how the battle for political power had come to focus on questions of competence rather than genuine ideological struggles between left and right. All this had begun to change rather abruptly with the election of Jeremy Corbyn as Labour leader in September 2015. Corbyn was committed to a series of radical policies, including nationalization of public utilities and unilateral nuclear disarmament.

Following the Referendum, the political landscape shifted still further. Theresa May was quick to draw the conclusion that there could be no return to business as usual. Her first speech as Prime Minister marked an abrupt departure from the language of David Cameron's austerity, and was peppered with references to 'burning injustice', to ordinary working-class families who can 'just about manage', and to a government 'driven not by the interests of the privileged few'.

The political rationale for this was all too obvious. Labour looked ripe for the taking. Its leader's popularity amongst his own members seemed inversely correlated with his appeal to the public at large (polling by Ipsos MORI in August 2016 revealed that even Theresa May was more popular with Labour supporters than Corbyn).[6] Substantively, the party struggled to come up with clear lines on either Brexit or immigration.

An enquiry carried out by Labour MP Jon Cruddas found that the party was losing socially conservative voters to UKIP. Yet UKIP's own travails continued. Its self-proclaimed role as 'guard dog of Brexit' hardly seemed necessary, given the Prime Minister's approach. And alongside the policy challenge was a financial one, as major donor Arron Banks walked away and – ironically enough – the party braced itself to lose the millions in salaries and allowances paid to its MEPs once Brexit occurred. In the 2015 General Election, UKIP had contested nearly every seat and won 13 per cent of the vote, making it the third-biggest party (although it only returned 1 MP). By 2017, for a variety of reasons, it contested only 377 seats out of 650.

As UKIP continued to implode, its voters were increasingly up for grabs. Little surprise, then, that the Prime Minister drove her tanks squarely into the middle of the Labour lawn. In an attempt to woo working-class Labour voters who might have defected to UKIP, a harsh tone was adopted on immigration, while, as we've seen, the Prime Minister made it clear she would proceed with Brexit. In her first speech as leader, she laid out a new economic agenda, based on using the power of government to 'stand up for the weak' and 'restore fairness', making the Conservatives the party of 'ordinary working-class people'. It was the first time any Conservative leader's speech had contained an explicit appeal to the working class since the middle of the last century.

Following her decision to call a snap election, these shifts in Conservative thinking crystallized still further. In both 2010 and 2015, political debate had centred round the need to reduce the deficit. In 2017, the Conservative manifesto was arguably the most statist and interventionist produced by a governing party in living memory. It declared that Conservatives 'do not believe in untrammelled free markets. We reject the cult of selfish individualism. We abhor social division, injustice, unfairness and inequality.' The *Spectator* magazine was moved to label Theresa May the most left-wing leader the Tories had had in perhaps forty years.

Labour made an even sharper break with its own recent past, proposing a massive expansion of state control of the economy, direct and indirect, including the reversal of several of the major Thatcher-era privatizations. Jeremy Corbyn built his own field of dreams. Politics was becoming ideological again.

The not so merry month for May

Ultimately, when it came to the election itself, personality was to matter as much as policy. Theresa May was quickly dubbed the 'Maybot', because of her Dalek-like repetition of the slogan 'strong and stable leadership'. Her rigid insistence that 'nothing has changed' after a screeching U-turn on social care further damaged her reputation. Conservative MPs looked on in horror as the virtues that were supposed to deliver a Tory landslide turned to vice.

In the event, it was Jeremy Corbyn – whose easy manner, passion and authenticity stood in stark contrast to Mrs May – who redeemed himself in the voters' eyes. He appeared a man reborn, buoyed by a surge of support from young people whose enthusiasm drew parallels with the US presidential campaign run by Bernie Sanders. Jez, it seemed, was feeling the Bern.

By following over 1,000 people every day throughout the campaign, the BES neatly captured both the nosedive in the Prime Minister's popularity and the equally striking rise in Corbyn's standing. The remarkable results are displayed in figure 5.1.[7] Such extensive swings in popularity had never previously been seen in an election campaign.

Equally, when it came to policy, after years of austerity, the Labour manifesto effectively tapped into a broad desire for change, promising more spending on public services, the NHS and education, and an end to university tuition fees.

Much has been made of Corbyn's ability to enthuse younger voters. And there is probably some truth to this

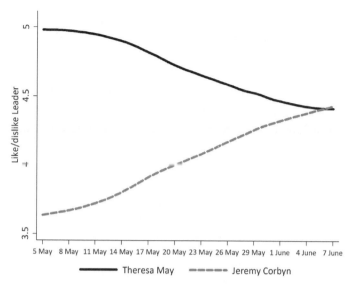

Figure 5.1 The popularity of the party leaders

Source: BES. Every day 1,000+ respondents rated the main party
leaders using a 10-point scale
(1 = strongly dislike, 10 = strongly like).

– though only some. Those aged 18 to 24 were three times more likely to vote Labour than Conservative. However, a post-election survey by YouGov found that, as ever, older people were much more likely to vote. Turnout amongst the over-70s was 84%, compared with 58% among 18- to 24-year-olds.

While the 'youth vote' was undoubtedly decisive in some university constituencies such as Canterbury, Sheffield Hallam and Cambridge, voters over the age of 40 were in fact far more important to Labour. More than half (54%) of those who voted for the party were aged 40 or over, compared with 46% who were younger – and only 26% who were under 30.

Above and beyond age, there was another crucial

driver of Labour support. Higher education became the party's new stronghold. Almost half (49%) of people with degree-level qualifications voted Labour, compared to only 33% of those with GCSEs or less.[8]

The link between these shifting voting patterns and the demographics underlying the Brexit vote are clear enough. The Remain vote shifted one way and the Leave (ex-UKIP) vote shifted another. The positions adopted by the parties towards this key issue were crucial in this regard. The Conservatives confidently expected to expand into Leave-voting Labour strongholds. And, as John Curtice points out, because Leave voters were disproportionately working class, it was in predominantly working-class constituencies that they advanced the most. Lord Ashcroft's polling shows that Conservative support was up 12 points from 2015 amongst working-class 'DE' voters, though only 4 points higher among professional and managerial 'AB' voters.[9] This helps explain the remarkable *volte-face* in Stoke-on-Trent South with which we opened this chapter.

But it was Labour and not the Conservatives who were ultimately better aligned with the electorate on Brexit. By moving the party towards the mildly eurosceptic centre – accepting the triggering of Article 50 and an end to freedom of movement – Corbyn managed to blunt the Conservatives' appeal in Leave-voting Labour areas, while capitalizing on growing alarm amongst Remainers at Theresa May's increasingly uncompromising hard-Brexit rhetoric.[10]

The net effect of this 'Brexit Blairism'[11] – or, perhaps more accurately, given the profound ambiguity of Labour's position, 'Brexit blurrism' – was startling. Labour benefitted from a swing across Remain areas

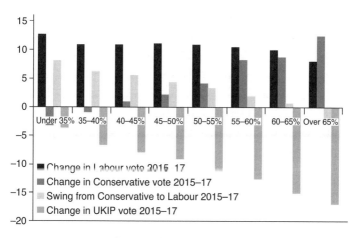

Figure 5.2 Vote changes from 2015 to 2017 by strength of Leave vote

Source: Ford, Goodwin and Sobolewska, 'British politics'.

sufficient to overturn huge Conservative majorities in Battersea, Kensington and Enfield Southgate, and to slash them in others, while remaining strong enough in Leave-voting Labour heartlands to prevent the Conservatives from turning too many of these seats blue. While the Conservatives gained most ground in the staunchest pro-Brexit seats (which also saw the biggest collapse in support for UKIP), they made just six gains from Labour in Leave areas of England and Wales.

Figure 5.2 illustrates the point nicely. Areas are ordered according to the proportion of their population that voted Leave in the Referendum, with the most 'Remain' areas on the left, and most 'Leave' areas on the right. Labour increased its vote from 2015 across the board.

The divisions revealed by the Referendum thus went on to shape the outcome of the General Election. Chris

Hanretty has estimated that Conservative support increased on average by 10 percentage points in constituencies where more than 60% voted Leave. In contrast, where the Leave vote was less than 45% it dropped by 2 percentage points. Labour's vote increased by 9 points even in Leave seats, but 12 points in Remain seats. Brexit had changed the shape of British politics quite fundamentally.

Three's a crowd

Between them, Labour and the Conservatives won no less than 82% of the votes in June 2017. The last time anything like this happened was in 1970: Harold Wilson versus Edward Heath, a World Cup in Mexico, and Britain still waiting to join the then European Community. Between 1979 and 2015, the figures for combined Labour and Conservative support at General Elections were: 81%, 70%, 73%, 76%, 74%, 73%, 67%, 65%, and 67%. The upward leap of 15% between 2015 and 2017 is unprecedented – as was so much in this election.

In part, this was because there was clear blue (red?) water between them. There was no triangulation or attempt to split differences. And while Theresa May tried her own reverse Blairite move (shifting leftwards on economic policy to attract Labour voters), Corbyn had scurried so far to the anti-austerity left that voters were confronted with a stark choice. When the big two offer real alternatives, the minor parties tend to lose out. The Green vote collapsed as its supporters went to Corbyn, to whom the Liberals also lost votes. UKIP supporters flocked largely (though not entirely) to May.[12]

The Shaping of Things to Come

Brexit appears to have paved the way for a return to a variant of the two-party politics that characterized the British political scene in the immediate post-war period. That said, however, the social and geographical distribution of Remain and Leave voters cut across the traditional class basis of Britain's old two-party system. We're left with a re-aligned two-party system, based not on class but on other demographic markers of values: education and age.

The Brexit effect

Brexit is reshaping our electoral politics. But it will also have an impact on the ability of politicians to deliver on the promises they've made. As we've seen, both major parties made ambitious promises and pledged to increase significantly the role of the state in the economy. Neither, in contrast, devoted any space to the potential implications of Brexit, preferring instead to focus on their commitment to securing a favourable deal for Britain from the EU.

So what, then, might Brexit mean? Clearly, we cannot know for certain. At the time of writing, negotiations with the EU have just started. How they pan out will be the key to any Brexit effect. There is still a real possibility that the talks will break down, that the UK will leave without an Article 50 'divorce' deal, let alone an agreement on future trade. Equally, Britain might negotiate a transitional deal with the EU that, in effect, prolongs its period of living under EU law, until a trade deal can be sorted out.

It is impossible to be specific about what Brexit might

imply without knowing what form Brexit might take. We can, however, make several informed speculations. The government remains committed to taking the country out of both the single market and the customs union. To understand what this might imply, we need to pause for a moment to consider what the economic forecasts have to say.

As we've seen, one of the consequences of the Referendum campaign was to make it easy for pro-Brexiters to pour scorn on these forecasts. The Treasury's short-term forecast was indeed wrong. However, to assume equivalence between the short- and long-term forecasts is, as Jonathan Portes has argued, akin to seeing weather and climate as analogous. While predicting the former is notoriously difficult, the science behind the latter is far more reliable. Equally, short-term economic forecasts, relying, essentially, on an ability to predict the short-term behaviour of millions of individuals interacting in a complex system, cannot be relied on. Forecasts concerning the long-term impact of Brexit, however, are based on a far more reliable body of economic thought grounded in robust methodologies. From this, two broad conclusions emerge. First, the longer-term forecasts are more likely to be accurate than their short-term brethren. Second, there is absolutely no logical reason to assume that, just because the latter have been proven inaccurate, the former will too.[13]

So, whatever the failings of the Treasury's short-term forecast, there is no reason not to take its long-term study seriously. This estimated that British GDP would be 3.4–4.3% lower in 2031 than it would have been had the UK remained in the EU, in the event that the country adopted the 'Norway option' of remaining in the European Economic Area. The figures for a bilateral trade agreement (the 'Canada option') and reliance on WTO terms were 4.6–7.8% and 5.4–9.5%, respectively.[14]

More recent figures envisage trade with the EU falling by some 40%, in the event that the UK leaves the single market and customs union. This would imply that GDP would be smaller by around 3% every year (or 2.4% net of savings from the cancellation of membership payments to the EU). In addition, foreign investment would fall by perhaps 20%. By contrast, the gains to be had from signing trade deals with other states look relatively meagre – a free-trade deal with the USA would lead to gains of something like 0.3% of GDP.[15]

We are not for a moment suggesting that this will all come to pass precisely as forecast. Economic forecasts are, of course, not always accurate. And while the methodology behind longer-term forecasts is robust, the simple fact of attempting to gaze so far into the future is intrinsically problematic. What we are saying, however, is that there is at least the possibility that Brexit will impact severely on the domestic economy. This would, apart from anything else, impose significant fiscal constraints on the government. The Treasury estimated that the Canada option would generate receipts £36 billion lower than in the case of EU membership by 2031 (more than a third of the NHS budget and the equivalent of 8p on the basic rate of income tax).

At the very least, then, it would have been prudent for the parties to factor a potential Brexit cost into their plans. None has done so. Nor has any of them been realistic about the ability of the state to pay for their ambitious election pledges as the Brexit process begins in earnest. Perhaps it is a legacy of the Referendum campaign that, following decades of centrist politics, our parties have decided that, as no-one seems to trust the experts anyway, economic forecasts can be easily ignored. We would suggest that this is a potentially damaging overcompensation.

Brexit will also provide the British state with arguably its most severe peace-time challenge. The Cabinet Secretary reckons it has few, if any, parallels in its complexity. And there are a number of different challenges to be confronted. There are the negotiations with the EU themselves, of course. And then there are the preparations for life after Brexit. These involve, among other things: a raft of legislation to pass (incorporating EU law into our law, and passing new laws in areas where Brexit will leave gaps – such as immigration and agriculture); relations with the devolved administrations to manage; and personnel to put in place to perform various functions either unnecessary whilst in the EU (customs checks) or currently performed by the Union (significant numbers of regulatory tasks). Some indication of the way the process will dominate our politics was provided by the Queen's Speech in June 2017. Eight of the twenty-seven bills it outlined are concerned solely with Brexit.

Whatever the ultimate outcome of Brexit, therefore, achieving it satisfactorily will present a massive challenge. Other policies might suffer as a result. To take but one topical example, a recent report suggested that one of the reasons a long-awaited review of building and safety regulations has not yet begun was that some civil servants were drafted away from it to deal with Brexit.[16] It is hard to see how resources will be available for the kinds of measures – such as improving skills and training – that might compensate for the impact of Brexit. One might legitimately, in other words, wonder whether the civil service will have the bandwidth to think about much else as Britain gears up for life outside the European Union. In June, news emerged that the Cabinet Secretary was planning to redeploy at least 750 policy experts from across Whitehall to key Brexit departments. And this, remember, is a civil service that has seen its numbers reduced from 480,000 full-time staff ahead of the 2010 spending review to 406,000 in March 2015.

Peering ahead

This is the context in which Mrs May's new minority administration must govern and attempt to implement its ambitious reform agenda. And she starts from a difficult position. On the plus side, GDP has been growing at around 2% since the Referendum, and the UK enjoyed the fastest growth of any G7 economy for 2016 as a whole – and even witnessed a rise in average earnings of 2.2%.

However, these figures conceal more worrying longer-term trends. The country has seen no productivity growth since the financial crisis. Indeed, ONS comparisons showed that its impact on productivity was twice as severe in the UK as in other G7 states.[17] Moreover, between 2008 and 2015, real wages fell by 1%, placing the UK 103rd out of a global ranking of 112 for real wage growth.[18] And in the first quarter of 2017, GDP growth fell to 0.2%. One reason for this was an inflation rate of nearly 3%, which has also meant that 'real' wages – that is to say, wages adjusted for inflation – are falling.

On top of this, there is the potential economic impact of a reduction in migration. The government has recommitted itself to a target for net migration in the tens of thousands – as opposed to the 273,000 recorded for the year to September 2016. This itself will have an impact on the economy, estimated by the Office for Budget Responsibility at some £6 billion a year by 2020–1. The IMF, for its part, has argued the hit could be worse still because of the impact on productivity growth.[19]

Moreover, as before the Referendum, some social groups were disproportionately affected by all of this. Following the Referendum, Theresa May pressed ahead with policies of freezing working-age benefits. And a report by the Resolution Foundation predicted an 'unprecedented' combination of weak average income growth and falling incomes for the entire bottom half of the working-age income distribution, producing the biggest rise in inequality since the Thatcher years. The depreciation of sterling seen since the Referendum has already disproportionately affected the lowest paid by pushing up food and fuel prices.[20] Moreover, the combination of low pay growth and benefit cuts means that the next four years (2016–17 to 2020–1) are 'on course to be even worse for the poorest third of households than the four years following the financial crisis'.[21]

This would hardly be a propitious environment for any government, let alone one committed, as this Prime Minister claims she is, to achieving both prosperity and fairness. Prevailing economic conditions, the possible impact of Brexit on the public finances, and the fact it will tie up civil service resources for some time to come make this a perhaps uniquely difficult moment to pursue such lofty ambitions.

Much, of course, will depend on how politics develops. It is, at the time of writing, far from clear that either the Prime Minister or the government will survive the Article 50 process that will end in March 2019.

Nor is it a given that either of the main parties will emerge unscathed from the Brexit process. A Conservative leadership election would blow open the simmering feud over Europe in its parliamentary party. Should the government stick to its guns and propel the country towards exit from both the single market and the customs union, it is hard to see, in the short term at least, how the Conservatives could maintain their reputation as a 'relatively' safe hand on the national economic tiller.

This matters all the more because indications are that it is precisely in those parts of the country where the Conservatives managed to appeal to Leave voters that the economic impact of reduced trade with the EU will hit hardest. In what can only be described as the profoundest of ironies, recent research reveals that those regions that voted strongly for Leave tend to be those most dependent on EU markets for their local economic development. They thus may well have the most to lose from the process, whilst the regions that voted Remain will be far less adversely affected.[22] The electoral consequences of an economically painful Brexit for the governing party are potentially severe.

As for Labour, the profound ambiguities in the party's position over both the single market and the customs union are striking. Ending free movement of people while retaining the economic benefits of membership sounds enticing, but is not something the European Union would ever offer. It may be that this contradiction is manageable in opposition. Simply attacking the government whilst failing to specify a clear possible alternative makes political sense.

But, again, we have to ask whether this will satisfy the party's electorate. As we write, there is a backlash underway from Remain supporters against the decision to whip MPs into voting against an amendment to the Queen's Speech in favour of customs union and single market membership. Whether Jeremy Corbyn can continue to appeal to both Leavers and Remainers – as he did so effectively during the General Election – is far from certain.

Then there is immigration. One of the less remarked on consequences of the Referendum was to undermine the status of immigration as one of the – if not the – most salient of political issues. The BES panel survey 'word clouds', showing what mattered to people during the 2017 campaign, were dramatically different from those shown in chapter 4. In 2016 immigration dominated for those who wanted to Leave. At no point in the 2017 campaign did the word immigration appear.[23] Likewise, the issue was hardly mentioned in the election campaign by the parties themselves and according to canvassers rarely came up in conversations on the doorstep.[24]

But this absence did not imply a lack of concern. It was merely that, for many voters, immigration was an issue that was, or was about to be, solved. Immigration itself had dropped markedly after 23 June 2016. And both parties made pledges to ensure numbers stayed down – the Conservatives (rather naively) reiterating their pledge to bring numbers down to the tens of thousands, and Labour promising to end freedom of movement.

Of course, as in so much else, Brexit was central. Voters might not have expressed concern about immigration – in the Ipsos issue-tracker survey of April 2017, Brexit came top of a list of the most important issues facing Britain (jointly, on 48 per cent, with the NHS).[25] However, a survey by the same company the previous month had revealed that 44 per cent of the electorate (and 63 per cent of Leave voters) saw an end to freedom of movement as the most important outcome of Brexit.[26] This lends some credence to the notion that the result of the EU Referendum was enough for voters to feel their voices had been heard and their concerns had been met.

What remains to be seen is how the immigration debate plays out. Given the positions of both major parties, it seems unlikely that any deal will be struck with the EU that does not end freedom of movement. That being said, the lesson we draw from the politics of the last eighteen months is that one should never say 'never'. There are clearly those within both parties who feel freedom of movement is a price worth paying for continued single market membership. And, of course, should a transitional deal be signed, to cover the period between the signing of an Article 50 deal and the conclusion of a trade deal, free movement may well remain in place for some years.

Even here, of course, there is a question as to whether people will want to continue to come to this country. The immigration figures suggest, as we have said, a fall in numbers already. With a devalued pound, uncertainty about the future, and the increased unattractiveness (to some, anyway) of living in a country that has rejected EU membership, it might be that ending free movement proves unnecessary.

This brings us back to the economics. As we've touched on above, cutting immigration will generate economic costs. And how the broader trade-off between Brexit and sustaining the economy is managed, we just do not know.

The fact there is uncertainty on this score at all underlines the degree to which politics has changed. Prior to the General Election, Theresa May broke with tradition by clearly prioritizing politics over economics. She privileged ending free movement and the jurisdiction of the European Court of Justice over the UK above considerations of any economic damage these decisions might imply. It is hard to overstate what a sea change this represented. Consensus politics involved close consultation with business leaders. What was good for the economy was deemed good for the country.[27]

A key question will be whether the present minority government will continue along the path set by a Prime Minister who appeared unchallengeable. Since the election, the government has given the impression of being more willing at least to consider the economic arguments. Previously, businesses would report that their pleas for a 'softer' Brexit to preserve trade with the EU had been largely ignored. Yet on 24 June 2017, the Prime Minister announced the creation of a Brexit Council involving ministers and key business representatives. Time will tell how the battle between Brexit politics and the British economy will play out.

What is clear, however, is that the electoral

consequences of the unfolding Brexit process will be significant. The Referendum opened the divisions in British society like bleeding sores. A survey by the relationship charity Relate found that one-fifth of their 300 counsellors had worked with clients arguing over Brexit.[28] And rebuilding British politics will take more than relationship counselling. A year after the Referendum, the British Election Study has found no sign of a decline in the strength of identification with the Leave and Remain camps. Indeed, these identities are currently far stronger than those associated with party support, as figure 5.3 underlines.

If Leave–Remain continues to be a schism in British politics and society, as it appears it might, there are real dangers for both major parties on the horizon.

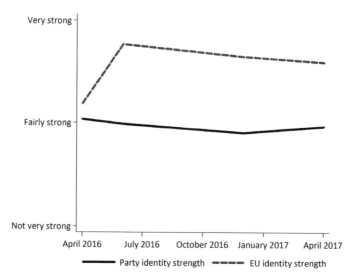

Figure 5.3 Leave and Remain: dominant new identities
Source: BES.[29]

What if . . . ?

As Britain moves towards the EU exit door, then, the political implications are only beginning to be felt. The pressure building to remove the public-sector pay cap is indicative of the problems the government will face in attempting to square a hugely complex economic circle. If Theresa May is still in office when any Brexit economic shock hits, Labour's softer line, combined with its popular economic policies, might, for all their ambiguities, enable the party to profit.

The volatile voters of modern Britain depicted in chapter 2 don't loyally stick by a party when they feel let down by it. There remains the possibility that a soft or stalled Brexit might provoke a resurgence of right-wing populism (though this clearly hinges crucially on whether public opinion turns against leaving the European Union). One (former) UKIP councillor, in a conversation with one of the authors, could hardly contain his glee at the thought of Brexit *not* working out: 'UKIP will rise again.'

Strong backers of Leave will certainly want to express their anger in the event that they feel betrayed. And if they do not turn to UKIP, then where? Disillusionment? Withdrawal from the political game altogether? Whatever transpires in the years to come, it will be difficult to maintain either the party system that emerged in June 2017 or the turnout accompanying it.

Either way, our politicians face a struggle in attempting to restore trust in politics, which, as we have seen, was so badly damaged prior to the Referendum. As Chris Deerin put it, characteristically bluntly:

The Shaping of Things to Come

The collapse of trust in our politicians, our politics, our institutions and our post-war settlement is real and it is profound. It pervades every layer of British society: every class, every income level, every age group and every ideological leaning. The titled, the humble and the dogs in the street alike know that our democracy has gone wonky.[30]

Pledges made and not delivered on are worse than those that never saw the light of day. Yet the promises made to us – of Brexit with increased prosperity and fairness – will be hard, if not impossible, to keep. Growing disillusionment and detachment remain a real possibility. And we know that people who lose the habit of voting don't usually rediscover it. The size of the electorate shrinks and the quality of our democracy shrinks with it.

Afterword: All Change – Brexit and British Politics

'Why should I do the hard shit for someone else, just to hand it over to them on a plate?' Theresa May might have felt this way since her ill-fated snap election in June. But the words are not hers. They were reportedly uttered by David Cameron to his inner circle when deciding on his future immediately after the EU Referendum.[1]

Having hummed contentedly to himself as he went back into 10 Downing Street, he went on, in a breathtaking display of hubris, to underline how little he knew or cared about the reasons for his humiliating defeat at the ballot box. In his resignation honours list, the Prime Minister rewarded leading Remain campaigners alongside party (and Remain) donors, political advisers, spin doctors, Cabinet ministers and his wife's hairdresser. Little surprise that the government was accused of giving a 'two fingered salute' to the public.[2] What really stuck in the craw of Leave campaigners and the wider public was the Prime Minister's willingness to reward those who, as Bill Cash put it, 'got it so completely wrong' on the Referendum.

Cameron's successor and the leader of the opposition both seemed to get it, however. The abrupt change in tone that followed Theresa May's election as Conservative leader, and the radical alternative laid out by Jeremy Corbyn, indicated that the lessons of the Referendum were clearer to them than they had been to the man who had called the vote in the first place.

Tone is not all that has changed. Politics since the Referendum has been characterized by what, on the surface, appears like a curious reversion to the past. The two-party system seems to have reasserted itself, while participation in politics is on the rise. And ideology is back. No more can our parties be accused of slugging it out over the political centre ground in dull, technocratic campaigns. Chants of 'Oh Jeremy Corbyn' at Glastonbury hardly indicate that a nascent crisis of democracy has been averted, but were indicative of a growing interest in politics among the young and – this was Glastonbury, after all – the not-so-young.

Yet appearances can be deceptive. All is not as it once was. For a start, as we've seen, the 2017 election hammered perhaps the final nail into the coffin of the class politics we had become so used to. As Labour flourished in middle-class Remain areas, so too did the Conservatives increase their vote share in working-class, Leave-leaning, constituencies. Both parties – particularly, but not only when it comes to Brexit – now resemble fragile coalitions whose stability is far from certain. And this new two-party system, of course, generated what it was never meant to – a minority government.

The election that everyone lost points to the fragility of the current state of affairs. Politics is in flux. We are living through one of those periodic moments when the tectonic plates of politics shift, and those affected strive to regain their balance.

One obvious question all this poses is whether it was always going to take something on the scale of the Referendum to shake up our increasingly dysfunctional system. There is a term for this. 'Punctuated equilibrium' is a concept that social scientists have borrowed from the study of evolutionary biology. What it means, (very) simply, is that, rather than change in any given system taking place gradually, via often painfully slow evolutionary processes, it comes about in short bursts. These bursts are precipitated by external shocks − be they changes to the natural environment that can lead to accelerated change in the species affected, or sudden shocks to political systems that can bring down or reform long-established structures.

The Referendum shattered the contemporary equilibrium of our politics. Not only did it bring down individual leaders, but it introduced a new divide in our society, with Leave–Remain coming to sit alongside the more traditional left–right division. The cosy centrist cartel − 'Remainia' to borrow Rafael Behr's felicitous phrase − that had competed for a reputation for competence, whilst broadly agreeing on the key ideas, was broken apart.

A positive reading of all this would be to see it as a necessary recalibration of a political system that was becoming unfit for purpose. For some, such as the *Spectator*'s Fraser Nelson, Brexit embodied the functionality of the British political system. The Referendum represented a 'safety valve' that effectively removed the need for voters to do something more drastic, such as electing their own version of President Trump.[3]

Yet there are few signs of the 'liberal insurgency' some Brexiters have claimed emerged from the Referendum.[4] Brexit, as we have shown, was largely, if not entirely, about reducing immigration. The policy responses of both major parties, with the rejection of free movement by Labour, and maintenance of an apparently random immigration target by the Conservatives, bear this out. Beyond vague rhetorical assertions about 'Global Britain', it is hard to see much that is open about the country today. And the anger that pervades the country in the wake of the Referendum is hardly redolent of a settled, liberal consensus.

Nonetheless, for those anxious to see the development of a fairer society, of a political system more receptive to and in touch with the desires of those it purports to represent, there were, perhaps, reasons to be cheerful in amongst all this. Corbyn's radicalism, along with the apparent rejection of the extremes of Thatcherism by the Conservatives, seemed to hold out the possibility of a new way of doing politics – a politics driven by a desire to redress the kinds of iniquities that had driven disillusion with the political system as the Referendum approached.

For some commentators, all this represents an electoral sea change that signals a rejection of neoliberalism and provides the possibility of 'a society intolerant of injustice and inequality'.[5] Outrage at the horrendous events at Grenfell Tower, and a willingness to link these to austerity policies, are taken as indicative of this new mood.

But, as we have seen, the voters have changed since the 1970s, when Keynesian orthodoxy was swept aside by the tide of neoliberalism. Today's electorate is composed of more volatile voters whose responses to politics are fast and furious and unlikely to change *en masse* in a single direction. So this speculative political recalibration rests on shaky foundations.

Stasis may have been overcome, but stability has not returned. Both major parties are riven by internal disagreements about Brexit and a host of other issues. Both leaders face unrest in their ranks. The Queen's Speech following the General Election of 2017 contained nothing to combat the numerous injustices the Prime Minister had been referring to for months, and which occupied pride of place in her manifesto. The new politics may yet turn out to be little more than new rhetoric.

The Referendum and its aftermath have already played a crucial role in reshaping the politics of this country. There is little reason to believe that the process of exiting the European Union will do otherwise. We are carrying out possibly the most important and complex set of peace-time negotiations ever. Carrying this out whilst the political tectonic plates are in movement will be challenging. Those charged with delivering Brexit bring to mind plate spinners struggling to keep their balance on a moving escalator.

Yet perhaps the most significant political impact of the Referendum is that it has ended the socially liberal, pro-market consensus that dominated UK politics for the last four decades. As Michael Ignatieff put it, when reviewing a book by the now ex-MP and former leader of the Liberal Democrats, Nick Clegg's 'brand of liberal moderation (and mine) is the natural mating call of elite cosmopolitans. The problem is that there just aren't enough cosmopolitans to win elections. Globalisation, open markets and European integration do not churn out enough winners to build stable electoral coalitions.'[6]

Unlike in General Elections over the last few decades, the Referendum gave the electorate a choice on these issues. It was one of those rare occasions when people voted in numbers and with conviction on a major question of policy they had the power to decide on. This was democracy as many believe it should be.

As we saw in chapter 5, the process of leaving the EU will impose enormous strain on the British state and may also impact severely on the public finances, at least in the short term. At the time of writing, given the sheer complexity of the Brexit process, and the profound uncertainty that surrounds politics at home, there is no way of knowing whether it can be successfully carried out or not. It is far from clear how long the Prime Minister can survive. Far from clear what stance our MPs will adopt towards their own leaders. Far from clear how they will choose to approach Brexit. And even less clear whether the legislation necessary to bring Brexit about can be passed.

If the process does not go well, it will lead some to reconsider our path. Even as we write these conclusions, more than fifty Labour politicians, including frontbenchers, have signed a statement claiming young voters had backed Labour because they wanted to 'stop the Tories in their tracks' over Brexit. They declared themselves 'unambiguously for membership of the single market'.

Equally, however, there are many for whom Brexit represents a triumph, almost regardless of its impact on the country. They are the political equivalent of those Leicester City fans who, drunk on the success of winning the Premier League title, felt, in the dark days of the following season, that relegation would be a price worth paying for that trophy. Albeit that the Brexiter's reward will not, of course, be a place in Europe.

The bitter divisions remain. And the divisive impact of the Referendum will generate a number of unintended and unanticipated consequences. Already, the political strain is beginning to tell. Both major parties are fundamentally divided over what to do next. We've mentioned the unrest generated within the Labour parliamentary party. Over the aisle, the mood is no less ugly. While one Conservative MP was referring to his pro-Brexit colleagues as 'fuckers', a member of the latter group was hitting out at threats from the 'wankers' on his party's other flank. As a *Financial Times* report put it, and in stark contrast to the remarks by David Cameron with which we opened this book, the 'poison is . . . running in the system'.[7]

How long it will continue to run for, we cannot be sure. But Brexit will continue to reshape our politics for the foreseeable future. And the echoes of its social and political impact will be present for decades to come.

Notes

Preface: That Was a Year, That Was

1 'David Cameron: Brexit vote ended a "poisoning" of UK politics', *Guardian*, 26 April 2017.

2 Andrew Marr, 'Anywheres vs Somewheres: the split that made Brexit inevitable', *New Statesman*, 17 March 2017.

3 Perhaps the best of these is Harold D. Clarke, Matthew Goodwin and Paul Whiteley, *Brexit: Why Britain Voted to Leave the European Union*, Cambridge University Press, 2017.

4 Tim Shipman, *All Out War: The Full Story of How Brexit Sank Britain's Political Class*, London: William Collins, 2016, p. xxv.

5 Ian Dunt, *Brexit: What the Hell Happens Now?* Tonbridge: Canbury Press, 2016; Daniel Hannan, *What Next: How to Get the Best from Brexit*, London: Head of Zeus, 2016.

1 The Best of Enemies

1 Simon Usherwood, 'Opposition to the European Union in the UK: the dilemma of public opinion and party

management', *Government and Opposition*, 37, 2 (2002), 211–30.

2 Helen Thompson, 'Inevitability and contingency: the political economy of Brexit', *The British Journal of Politics and International Relations*, 19, 3 (2017), 434–49.

3 UK Polling Report, *Voting Intention since 2010*, http://ukpollingreport.co.uk/voting-intention-2.

4 Quoted in the *Financial Times*, 24 June 2016.

5 Geoffrey Evans and Jonathan Mellon, 'Immigration and euroscepticism: the rising storm', *Guardian*, 18 December 2015, https://www.theguardian.com/news/datablog/2015/dec/18/immigration-euroscepticism-rising-storm-eu-referendum.

6 C. Dustmann, M. Casanova, M. Fertig, I. Preston and C. M. Schmidt, *The Impact of EU Enlargement on Migration Flows*, Home Office Online Report 25/03, London: Research Development and Statistics Directorate, Home Office, 2003.

7 These figures differ somewhat from estimates using the International Passenger Survey. However, all studies agree that the number of immigrants from the accession countries exceeded the Home Office estimates by many multiples.

8 C. Vargas-Silva and Y. Markaki, *EU Migration to and from the UK*, Migration Observatory Briefing, COMPAS, University of Oxford, 2015.

9 Ipsos MORI, General Election Panel Survey, Wave 1, 1997, https://ipsos-rsl.com/researchpublications/research archive/2158/1997-General-Election-Panel-Survey-Wave-1.aspx.

10 Roger Mortimore, *Polling History: 40 Years of British Views on 'In or Out' of Europe*, June 2016, http://thecon versation.com/polling-history-40-years-of-british-views-on-in-or-out-of-europe-61250.

11 See House of Commons Library, 'Leaving the EU', Research Paper 13/42, 1 July 2013, p. 4.

12 Geoffrey Evans, Noah Carl, James Dennison, 'Brexit: the causes and consequences of the UK's decision to leave the EU', in Manuel Castells et al., eds., *Europe's Crises*, Cambridge: Polity, 2017, pp. 380–404.

13 https://www.ipsos.com/ipsos-mori/en-uk/ipsos-mori-exp enses-poll-bbc.

14 The black line summarizes the relationship between EU disapproval and concern about immigration. The grey band describes the broad area the relationship falls within (with 95% confidence).

15 Detailed information from the Continuous Monitoring Survey is not publicly available after 2013.

16 Tim Shipman, *All Out War: The Full Story of How Brexit Sank Britain's Political Class*, London: William Collins, 2016, pp. 15–17.

17 The Conservative Party Manifesto 2015: 'Strong leadership; a clear economic plan; a brighter, more secure future', https://s3-eu-west-1.amazonaws.com/manifesto 2015/ConservativeManifesto2015.pdf, p. 30.

18 Stephen Bush, 'Westminster has yet to come to terms with the consequences of Brexit', *The New Statesman*, 2 July 2016.

2 Broken Politics

1 Colin Hay, *Why We Hate Politics*, London: Polity, 2007.

2 These figures were calculated by Chris Prosser using the manifesto data collected and coded by Ian Budge and his colleagues across all elections from 1945 as part of the Comparative Manifesto Project.

3 Peter Mair, *Ruling the Void: The Hollowing of Western Democracy*, London: Verso, 2013, p. 68.

4 Cas Mudde, 'Europe's populist surge', *Foreign Affairs*, Nov./Dec. 2016, 27.

5 Bridget Christie, '650 million reasons to dislike Andrew Lloyd Webber', *The Guardian*, 7 November 2015, https://www.theguardian.com/lifeandstyle/2015/nov/07/andrew-lloyd-webber-tax-credit-cuts-bridget-christie.

6 Jane Green and Will Jennings, *The Politics of Competence: Parties, Public Opinion and Voters*, Cambridge University Press, 2017.

7 Geoffrey Evans and James Tilley, *The New Politics of Class: The Political Exclusion of the British Working Class*, Oxford University Press, 2017, p. 131.

8 Ibid., pp. 120–2. These trends are obtained by content analysing all manifestos and leaders' speeches delivered by the Conservative and Labour parties since 1945 for references to the working class and families. For this we thank Chris Prosser of the BES.

9 *Independent*, 28 July 2014.

10 Ibid., pp. 126–30.

11 The best study on this topic is by Nick Carnes in the USA: Nicholas Carnes, 'Does the numerical underrepresentation of the working class in congress matter?' *Legislative Studies Quarterly*, 37, 1 (2012), 5–34.

12 Rosie Campbell and Philip Cowley, 'What voters want: reactions to candidate characteristics in a survey experiment', *Political Studies*, 62, 4 (2014), 745–65.

13 Alan S. Blinder, 'Is government too political?' *Foreign Affairs*, Nov./Dec. 1997, 115–26.

14 Frank Fischer, *Technocracy and the Politics of Expertise*, Newbury Park, CA: Sage, 1990, p. 35.

15 Quoted by Hay, *Why We Hate Politics*, p. 93.

16 See the discussion in ibid., ch. 4.

17 See Mair, *Ruling the Void*, pp. 115, 118.

18 B. Henderson, 'Huge turnout of 72.2 per cent for EU referendum with 33.6 million voting', *Daily Telegraph*, 24

June 2016, www.telegraph.co.uk/news/2016/06/23/high-turnout-for-eu-referendum-vote-could-break-uk-records.

19 N. Barker, 'Apathy in the UK? A look at the attitudes of non-voters', *Survation*, http://survation.com/apathy-in-the-uk-understanding-the-attitudes-of-non-voters.

20 National Centre of Social Research, 'Introduction', *British Social Attitudes 33*, 2016, www.bsa.natcen.ac.uk/latest-report/british-social-attitudes-33/introduction.aspx.

21 E. Fieldhouse, J. Green, G. Evans, J. Mellon, C. Prosser, H. Schmitt and C. van der Eijk, *The Volatile Voter: Shocks, Constraint, and the Destabilization of British Politics*, Oxford University Press, 2018. These figures were obtained from the BES post-election surveys conducted following every General Election since 1964.

22 Ibid. These figures were obtained from the BES panel surveys (which follow the same people through time, rather than asking new people with each wave of the survey), conducted across most General Election cycles since 1964.

23 Evans and Tilley, *The New Politics of Class*, pp. 170–7.

24 From M. Flinders, 'Low voter turnout is clearly a problem, but a much greater worry is the growing inequality of that turnout', LSE British Politics and Policy Blog, 13 March 2014, http://blogs.lse.ac.uk/politicsandpolicy/look-beneath-the-vote; Geoffrey Evans and James Tilley, 'The new class war: excluding the working class in 21st-century Britain', *Juncture*, 21, 4 (2015), 265–71.

25 https://www.ippr.org/publications/divided-democracy-political-inequality-in-the-uk-and-why-it-matters.

26 Ipsos MORI, 'Expenses poll for the BBC', 2 June 2009, https://www.ipsos-mori.com/Assets/Docs/SRI_Politics_BBCExpenses_Topline.PDF.

27 www.telegraph.co.uk/news/8197672/British-Social-Attitudes-survey-trust-in-politics-hits-new-low-over-MPs-expenses-scandal.html, and www.bsa-data.natcen.ac.uk.

Going even further back, Will Jennings and Gerry Stoker examined public beliefs about 'What motivates politicians?' from as far back as the 1940s. In 1944 and in 1972, a substantial proportion of voters believed politicians were looking out for their country (36% and 28%, respectively) but that had fallen to just 10% by 2014: https://sotonpolitics.org/2015/01/19/the-impact-of-anti-politics-on-the-uk-general-election-2015.

28 Swati Dhingra, 'Salvaging Brexit: the right way to leave the EU', *Foreign Affairs*, Nov./Dec. 2016, 90–100.

29 J. Browne and W. Elming, 'The effect of the coalition's tax and benefit changes on household incomes and work incentives', Institute for Fiscal Studies Briefing Note BN159.

30 'Political disaffection is rising, and driving UKIP support', https://yougov.co.uk/news/2014/10/29/political-disaffec tion-not-new-it-rising-and-drivi.

31 Geoffrey Evans and Jonathan Mellon, 'Identity, awareness and political attitudes: why are we still working class?' *British Social Attitudes 33*, 2016, www.bsa.natcen.ac.uk/ latest-report/british-social-attitudes-33/social-class.aspx.

32 Yougov / *The Times*, https://d25d2506sfb94s.cloudfront .net/cumulus_uploads/document/wwqytvw1lq/YG-Arch ive-150325-TheTimes.pdf.

33 Mudde, 'Europe's populist surge', 25–30.

34 Yascha Mounk, 'The week democracy died', *Slate.com*, 14 August 2016, www.slate.com/articles/news_and_poli tics/cover_story/2016/08/the_week_democracy_died_ how_brexit_nice_turkey_and_trump_are_all_connected. html.

35 'Political disaffection is rising, and driving UKIP support', https://yougov.co.uk/news/2014/10/29/political-disaffec tion-not-new-it-rising-and-drivi.

36 'MPs' expenses: Lord Tebbit says do not vote Conservative at European elections', *Daily Telegraph*, 12 May 2009.

37 'Fringe parties gain ground in scandal-hit Britain',

Reuters, 18 May 2009, www.reuters.com/article/britain-politics-expenses-idUSLI27559520090518?sp=true.

38 Manuel Funke, Moritz Schularick and Christoph Trebesch, 'Politics in the slump: polarization and extremism after financial crises, 1870–2014', http://ec.europa.eu/economy_finance/events/2015/20151001_post_crisis_slump/documents/c._trebesch.pdf.

39 www.bsa.natcen.ac.uk/media/39196/bsa34_full-report_fin.pdf, p. 45.

40 www.ipsos-mori-generations.com/Death-Penalty.

41 James Dennison and Matthew Goodwin, 'Immigration, issue ownership and the rise of UKIP', *Britain Votes 2015*, Hansard Society Series in Politics and Government, Oxford University Press, September 2015.

42 Quoted in the *Guardian*, 28 February 2014.

43 Hansard Society, *Audit of Political Engagement 9*, London: Hansard Society, 2012, p. 1, https://assets.contentful.com/xkbace0jm9pp/3N7Lqnn5LqkIMwME8qGqkq/6dc9bd63b2c615785da892caa7d421f5/Audit_of_Political_Engagement_9_-_Part_One__2012_.pdf.

44 Ibid., p. 4.

45 Hansard Society, *Audit of Political Engagement 10*, London: Hansard Society, 2013, p. 1, https://assets.contentful.com/xkbace0jm9pp/FxyrysDnMYQkKKsqkiaIE/1fb8b7058ff4005bb8f7dc64e5d9d5c5/Audit_of_Political_Engagement_10__2013_.pdf.

46 Mair, *Ruling the Void*, pp. 1, 2.

3 The Referendum

1 Paul Stephenson, 'How to win a referendum', *Politico*, 9 December 2016, www.politico.eu/article/how-to-win-a-referendum-brexit-inside-story-vote-leave-campaign.

2 www.consilium.europa.eu/uedocs/cms_data/docs/pressdata/en/ec/143478.pdf, p. 11.

3 Survey carried out by The UK in a Changing Europe, http://ukandeu.ac.uk/a-third-of-mps-still-undecided-which-way-they-will-vote-in-the-uks-eu-referendum-new-poll-shows.

4 Survey carried out by *The UK in a Changing Europe*, http://ukandeu.ac.uk/profound-divisions-among-mps-over-brexit-survey-reveals/.

5 Tim Shipman, *All Out War: The Full Story of How Brexit Sank Britain's Political Class*, London: William Collins, 2016, p. 175.

6 Katrin Bennhold, 'To understand "Brexit," look to Britain's tabloids', *New York Times*, 2 May 2017.

7 Peter Mandelson, 'How the struggle for Europe was lost', *Financial Times*, 2 July 2016.

8 Sunder Katwala, 'Is Nigel Farage hurting the eurosceptic cause?' *New Statesman*, 3 April 2014.

9 'Michael Gove: Why I'm backing Brexit', *Spectator*, 20 February 2016, http://blogs.spectator.co.uk/2016/02/michael-gove-why-im-backing-leave.

10 *Financial Times*, 18 December 2016.

11 Rafael Behr, 'How Remain failed: the inside story of a doomed campaign', *Guardian*, 5 July 2016, www.theguardian.com/politics/2016/jul/05/how-remain-failed-inside-story-doomed-campaign.

12 *Daily Telegraph*, 20 February 2016.

13 Tim Shipman puts this down to tiredness after the designation battle, or over-confidence: *All Out War*, p. 225.

14 Fraser Nelson, 'In this topsy-turvy world, Remainers have become the illiberal Brexit enforcers, whether Leavers like it or not', *Daily Telegraph*, 6 October 2016.

15 'Michael Gove claims migration will fall to "tens of thousands" after Brexit', *PoliticsHome*, 5 June 2016, https://www.politicshome.com/news/europe/eu-policy-agenda/brexit/news/75765/michael-gove-claims-migration-will-fall-tens.

16 Quoted in the *Guardian*, 26 May 2016.
17 *Sunday Times*, 29 May 2016.
18 'Boris bumbles at Brexit debutante ball', *Politico*, 26 May 2016.
19 *Daily Telegraph*, 14 May 2016.
20 YouGov survey with fieldwork conducted 9–10 June 2016. Full data available at https://d25d2506sfb94s. cloudfront.net/cumulus_uploads/document/qi3olqsp2n/ SundayTimesResults_160610_EUReferendum.pdf.
21 See https://www.gov.uk/government/publications/hm-tre asury-analysis-the-long-term-economic-impact-of-eu-me mbership-and-the-alternatives.
22 https://www.gov.uk/government/news/britain-to-enter-recession-with-500000-uk-jobs-lost-if-it-left-eu-new-trea sury-analysis-shows.
23 Aditya Chakrabortty, 'One blunt heckler has revealed just how much the UK economy is failing us', *Guardian*, 10 January 2017.
24 Jonathan Portes, 'Spreadsheets are people too: statistics and reality', http://notthetreasuryview.blogspot.co.uk/ 2017/04/spreadsheets-are-people-too-statistics.html.
25 Shipman, *All Out War*, p. 251.
26 John Curtice, 'Brexit reflections – how the polls got it wrong again', Centre on Constitutional Change, 28 June 2016, www.centreonconstitutionalchange.ac.uk/blog/ brexit-reflections-how-polls-got-it-wrong-again.
27 Behr, 'How Remain failed'.
28 Quoted in the *Financial Times*, 18 December 2016.
29 Stephenson, 'How to win a referendum'.
30 Boris Johnson, 'Do Bremainers really think voters will be cowed by the likes of Obama?' *Daily Telegraph*, 24 April 2016, www.telegraph.co.uk/news/2016/04/24/ do-bremainers-really-think-voters-will-be-cowed-by-the-likes-of.
31 Boris Johnson, 'Of course our City fat cats love the EU

– it's why they earn so much', *Daily Telegraph*, 15 May 2016, www.telegraph.co.uk/news/2016/05/15/of-course-our-city-fat-cats-love-the-eu--its-why-they-earn-so-mu.

32 Paul Waugh, 'Jeremy Corbyn allies "sabotaged" Labour's in campaign on the EU referendum, critics claimed', Huffington Post UK, 25 June 2016, www.huffingtonpost.co.uk/entry/jeremy-corbyn-allies-sabotaged-labour-in-campaign-and-fuelled-brexit_uk_576eb1b5e4b 0d2571149bb1f.

33 Politico, 'How David Cameron blew it', www.politico. eu/article/how-david-cameron-lost-brexit-EU-referendum -prime-minister-campaign-remain-Boris-Craig-Oliver- Jim-Messine-Obama.

34 Behr, 'How Remain failed'.

35 Ibid.

4 Voting to Leave

1 Peter Mair, *Ruling the Void: The Hollowing of Western Democracy*, London: Verso, 2013, p. 114, fn. 6.

2 Geoffrey Evans and Christopher Prosser, 'Was it always a done deal? The relative impact of short- and long-term influences on referendum voting', BES Working Paper.

3 Kirby Swales, 'Understanding the Leave vote', NatCen, December 2016, http://natcen.ac.uk/media/1319222/ natcen_brexplanations-report-final-web2.pdf.

4 Evans and Prosser, 'Was it always a done deal?'

5 https://european.economicblogs.org/lse/2016/blogadmin- polls-referendum.

6 http://lordashcroftpolls.com/2016/06/how-the-united- kingdom-voted-and-why.

7 Chris Prosser, Jon Mellon and Jane Green, 'What mattered most to you when deciding how to vote in the EU referendum?' 2016, www.britishelectionstudy.com/

bes-findings/what-mattered-most-to-you-when-deciding-how-to-vote-in-the-eu-referendum/#.WVeTO7pFyF4.

8 Sascha O. Becker, Thiemo Fetzer and Dennis Novy, 'Who voted for Brexit? A comprehensive district-level analysis', CEP Discussion Paper No. 1480, April 2017, p. 19.

9 Ibid., p. 32.

10 Ibid., p. 29.

11 www.independent.co.uk/news/uk/politics/eu-referen dum-polls-remain-stay-brexit-david-cameron-who-will-win-a7090111.html.

12 Peter Kellner, 'Don't celebrate too soon, Brexiters. History favours Remain', *New Statesman*, 6 June 2016, www. newstatesman.com/politics/elections/2016/06/dont-cele brate-too-soon-brexiters-history-favours-remain.

13 See p. 54, above.

14 www.conservativehome.com/thecolumnists/2016/06/ daniel-hannan-%E2%80%8Bthere-are-no-qualified-rem ain-votes-voting-leave-is-the-only-way-to-avoid-eu-inte gration.html.

15 Geoffrey Evans and James Tilley, *The New Politics of Class: The Political Exclusion of the British Working Class*, Oxford University Press, 2017, p. 205. See also M. Goodwin and O. Heath, 'The 2016 Referendum, Brexit and the left behind: an aggregate-level analysis of the result', *The Political Quarterly*, 87, 3 (2016), 323–32.

16 Evans and Tilley, *The New Politics of Class*, p. 205.

17 Swales, 'Understanding the Leave vote'.

18 Ibid.

19 https://www.theguardian.com/commentisfree/2016/jun/ 09/michael-gove-experts-academics-vote.

20 Evans and Tilley, *The New Politics of Class*, p. 202.

21 Eric Kaufmann, 'It's NOT the economy, stupid: Brexit as a story of personal values', British Politics and Policy at LSE, 2016, http://blogs.lse.ac.uk/politicsandpolicy/per sonal-values-brexit-vote.

22 Evans and Tilley, *The New Politics of Class*, ch. 4.
23 C. Dustmann, T. Frattini and I. Preston, 'The effect of immigration along the distribution of wages', *The Review of Economic Studies*, 80 (2013), 145–73; S. Nickell and J. Saleheen, 'The impact of immigration on occupational wages: evidence from Britain', Bank of England Staff Working Paper No. 574, 2015.
24 Evans and Tilley, *The New Politics of Class*, p. 202.
25 See, amongst many, www.independent.co.uk/voices/eu-referendum-brexit-young-people-upset-by-the-outcome-of-the-eu-referendum-why-didnt-you-vote-a7105396.html. Goodwin and Heath, 'The 2016 Referendum', provides academic back-up.
26 Becker et al., 'Who voted for Brexit?', pp. 31–2.
27 Ashcroft's poll found that those aged 35–44 voted Remain (52% in favour); beyond that age, Leave dominated: lordashcroft.com, June 2016.
28 Swales, 'Understanding the Leave vote', p. 2.
29 Sara B. Hobolt, 'The Brexit vote: a divided nation, a divided continent', *Journal of European Public Policy*, 23, 9 (2016), 1270.

5 The Shaping of Things to Come

1 House of Commons, Public Administration and Constitutional Affairs Committee, *Lessons Learned from the EU Referendum*, Twelfth Report of Session 2016–17, HC 496, 12 April 2017, para. 168.
2 House of Commons, Foreign Affairs Committee, *Equipping the Government for Brexit*, Second Report of Session 2016–17, HC 431, 20 July 2016, p. 3.
3 www.bbc.co.uk/news/uk-politics-eu-referendum-36457120.
4 https://d25d2506sfb94s.cloudfront.net/cumulus_uploads/document/l094qb1ds4/InternalResults_170508_Releavers_W.pdf.

5 www.standard.co.uk/news/politics/support-for-brexit-so
ars-as-theresa-may-triggers-article-50-a3502156.html.

6 http://uk.businessinsider.com/ipsos-mori-poll-theresa-ma
y-jeremy-corbyn-2016-8.

7 Thanks to Chris Prosser of the BES for supplying this figure.

8 https://yougov.co.uk/news/2017/06/13/how-britain-vot
ed-2017-general-election.

9 John Curtice, 'Brexit and the election', http://ukandeu.
ac.uk/wp content/uploads/2017/06/One-year-on.pdf.

10 Robert Ford, Matthew Goodwin and Maria Sobolewska, 'British politics', http://ukandeu.ac.uk/wp-content/uplo
ads/2017/06/One-year-on.pdf.

11 Ibid.

12 Thanks to Jon Mellon for providing us with these analyses from the 2017 BES.

13 Jonathan Portes, 'Weather is not climate: forecasting the impacts of Brexit', http://ukandeu.ac.uk/weather-is-not-climate-forecasting-the-impacts-of-brexit.

14 HM Treasury, 'HM Treasury analysis: the long-term economic impact of EU membership and the alternatives', April 2016, https://www.gov.uk/government/uploads/
system/uploads/attachment_data/file/517415/treasury_
analysis_economic_impact_of_eu_membership_web.pdf.

15 Swati Dhingra, 'UK economic policy', http://ukandeu.
ac.uk/wp-content/uploads/2017/05/Red-Yellow-and-
Blue-Brexit-The-Manifestos-Uncovered.pdf.

16 'Revealed: the tower block fire warnings that ministers ignored', *Guardian*, 17 June 2017.

17 https://www.theguardian.com/business/2016/feb/18/uk-
productivity-gap-widens-to-worst-level-since-records-be
gan.

18 http://touchstoneblog.org.uk/2017/02/uk-103rd-112-
global-ranking-real-wage-growth-since-crisis.

19 Jonathan Portes, 'Brexit, migration and the UK economy',

http://ukandeu.ac.uk/brexit-migration-and-the-uk-econ omy.

20 'A bleak outlook for UK living standards', *Financial Times*, 5 February 2017.

21 Resolution Foundation, 'Are we nearly there yet? Spring Budget 2017 and the 15-year squeeze on family and public finance', March 2017, www.resolutionfoundation.org /app/uploads/2017/03/Spring-Budget-2017-response.pdf.

22 Bart Los, Philip McCann, John Springford and Mark Thissen, 'The mismatch between local voting and the local economic consequences of Brexit', *Regional Studies*, 512, 5 (2017), 786–99.

23 Thanks to Chris Prosser of the BES for providing this information.

24 Helen Lewis, 'What drove Labour's success? A tough line on immigration, and an appeal to the middle class', 12 June 2017, *New Statesman*, www.newstatesman.com/ politics/june2017/2017/06/what-drove-labours-success-tough-line-immigration-and-appeal-middle-class.

25 https://www.slideshare.net/IpsosMORI/ipsos-mori-issu es-index-april-2017.

26 Ipsos MORI, 'Four in ten have confidence in May to get a good deal for Britain in Brexit negotiations', 17 March 2017, https://www.ipsos.com/ipsos-mori/en-uk/four-ten-have-confidence-may-get-good-deal-britain-brexit-negoti ations.

27 Anand Menon and Camilla Macdonald, 'Can the Brexit denial finally stop now?' *Foreign Policy*, 29 March 2017, http://foreignpolicy.com/2017/03/29/can-the-brexit-den iers-finally-shut-up-now.

28 'Brexit arguments causing rifts between couples, coun sellors say', *Independent*, 29 December 2016, www. independent.co.uk/news/uk/home-news/brexit-anxieties-issue-troubled-couples-relationship-counsellors-experts-a7500876.html.

29 We would like to thank Chris Prosser of the BES for this figure.

30 Chris Deerin, *The Herald Scotland*, 4 July 2017, www. heraldscotland.com/news/15386597.Chris_Deerin__Thi s_growing_gap_between_the_governed_and_the_govern ing.

Afterword: All Change – Brexit and British Politics

1 *Daily Telegraph*, 25 June 2016.

2 'Cronyism pure and simple: David Cameron under fire for resignation honours list', *Sun*, 1 August 2016, https://www.thesun.co.uk/news/1531602/david-cameron -under-fire-for-resignation-honours-list-full-of-tory-chu ms-and-even-his-wifes-hairdresser.

3 'Why Trump's victory isn't like Brexit', *Spectator*, 12 November 2016, https://www.spectator.co.uk/2016/11/ why-trumps-victory-isnt-like-brexit.

4 Douglas Carswell, 'Leaving the EU is the start of a liberal insurgency', *Guardian*, 5 March 2017.

5 Owen Jones, 'The old Tory order is crumbling – it's taken Grenfell for us to really see it', *Guardian*, 22 June 2017.

6 'Michael Ignatieff on the lessons for liberals in Nick Clegg's memoir', *Financial Times*, 7 September 2016, https://www.ft.com/content/baee9688-743a-11e6-bf48- b372cdb1043a.

7 https://www.ft.com/content/02f15952-6099-11e7-8814- 0ac7eb84e5f1.

Index

140

Index

Index

education
  2017 election and, 101
  of MPs, 29
  Referendum vote and, 84
  voter values and, 77–8
  voting behaviour and, 34–5
Einstein, Albert, 59
Elliott, Matthew, 58, 64
Enfield Southgate
  2017 Labour vote, 103
European Coal and Steel
  Community (ECSC), 2
European Commission, 12
European Communities Act of
  1972 (UK)
  sovereignty issue and, 12
European Community (EEC)
  UK joins, 2–3
  see also European Union (EU)
European Court of Justice (ECJ)
  irritation to UK lawmakers,
    55
  May and, 114
European Economic Area
  'Norway' model, 60, 106–7
European Exchange Rate
  Mechanism (ERM), x
  UK's Black Wednesday and,
    5
European People's Party
  Cameron and, 22–3
European Union (EU)
  ban on British beef, 6
  Cameron's renegotiation,
    9–10, 47–8, 80
  Constitutional Treaty
    ratification, 8
  financial contributions to, 3
  globalization and, 32–3
  integration, 80
  single market models, 93–4
  supranational principle, 12
  UK opposes further
    integration, 4–6
European Union Act (UK), 8

euroscepticism
  historical perspective on,
    1–10
  pressure for Referendum,
    xii
  values and, 71–8
  see also Leave campaign
eurozone
  Brown resists joining, 6
  crisis, xii–xiii, 5, 7, 8
  see also Greece, austerity in
Evans, Suzanne, 92
experts
  Leave attacks on, 62–3
  not trusted, 108

Falconer, Charles, Lord
  Falconer of Thoroton, 31
Farage, Nigel
  attacks Blair, 13
  with Boris Johnson in pocket,
    64
  on integration, 80
  Labour Leavers and, 67
  Leave campaign's distancing
    attempt, 52
  migrant issue and, 42–3
  resigns leadership, 90, x
  role in campaign, xiii
  surprised by vote, ix–x
  UKIP successes, 10
financial crisis of 2008
  Eurozone and, 7
  ongoing effect in UK,
    109–10
  populist politics and, 40
  slow recovery from, 37
Financial Times, 124
Fiscal Compact Treaty, 23
Fox, Liam, 92
France
  formation of ECSC, 2
  identity as European, 18
  Zhou on French Revolution,
    xv

Index

Index

Index

Index

Index